Otis Redding's extraordinary voice resonates down the years profound beauty and u emotional depth. His unique vocal delivery gave Motown's pop artists a run for their money, while his stage presence matched pioneering funk magus – and fellow Georgia native – James Brown for sheer entertainment value. Crucial to the success of the Stax label, Redding quickly rose from obscurity and, thanks to his dizzying performance at the Monterey Pop Festival in 1967, was poised for major crossover success.

However, on December 10, 1967, he was killed when his private plane crashed into Lake Monoma near Madison, Wisconsin. '(Sittin' On) The Dock of the Bay', recorded just a week earlier, went straight to Number 1, prompting widespread speculation on what Otis Redding might have achieved had his life not been cut brutally short.

In this, the first serious profile of the soul legend, Geoff Brown talks to Stax illuminati Booker T. Jones, Isaac Hayes and David Porter, plus many others, about his tragically brief life, infectious personality and incredible talent. The resulting biography is a wonderful testament to this greatly loved artist.

OTIS REDDING

Otis Redding

Try A Little Tenderness

GEOFF BROWN

3

First published in the UK and simultaneously in North America
in 2001 by MOJO Books, an imprint of Canongate Books,
14 High Street, Edinburgh EH1 1TE

10 9 8 7 6 5 4 3 2 1

British Library Cataloguing-in-Publication Data
A catalogue record for this book is available on request
from the British Library

ISBN 1 84195 086 6

Typeset by Patty Rennie Production, Glenbervie
Printed and bound by Grafos, Spain

www. canongate.net

Contents

Acknowledgements   vi

1   Monterey – Stax Tops The Pops   1

2   Macon – Home In Your Heart   7

3   Memphis – Soul Stew   20

4   McLemore Magic   35

5   Otis Blue   57

6   The Soul Lexicographer   78

7   Soul Invasion – Otis In Europe   113

8   Madison, Wisconsin – Dreams To Remember   132

9   Amen   144

Timeline   160

Bibliography   164

Discography   165

Acknowledgements

THANKS TO THE MANY FOLKS IN TENNESSEE, Georgia and California who made me welcome and shared their memories of Otis and to those who gave up time when passing through London – or on the end of a transatlantic phone. I must thank in particular Wayne Jackson, Isaac Hayes, Booker T. Jones, Steve Cropper, Rufus Thomas, Sam Moore, Percy Sledge, Ben Cauley, Andrew Love, Barry Dickins, Andy Neill and Pat Gilbert. Thanks too, to Kieran and Erica O'Rourke for putting me up in Los Angeles, but most of all to Catherine, Rebecca and Ella for putting up with me in Highbury, Richmond, Oxford, Muswell Hill and wherever else we end up next.

1 Monterey – *Stax Tops the Pops*

ON JUNE 17, 1967, BUSY AND BEAMING, OTIS
Redding stormed on to the stage of the Monterey
International Pop Festival like a benign hurricane, and in
not much more than 20 minutes had whipped up and
wrung out the white hippy crowd. Few of them could have
known what was about to hit them when, after the Stax
house band had played three instrumentals, Tommy
Smothers introduced the singer. Otis strode on, a dominating presence in black sweater and a shiny, beige-green
suit barely containing his big frame – "He looked 12 or 14
feet tall," Bob Weir of The Grateful Dead recalled – and
drove into a thunderous version of Sam Cooke's Shake,

followed by his own classic uptempo anthem Respect. He made no concessions to winning over this new audience, one he'd later call "The Love Crowd", he just gave his all, as usual, and the sheer force of his personality and music did the rest. Not a graceful mover, he stomped his feet in approximation of a dance as the hard-driving, emotionally uncorrupted music swept over the crowd like a force of nature.

"On stage was just one of those times when you could feel all the energy and the electricity," Booker T. Jones, keyboard-player with the MG's remembers. "I think we did one of our best shows, Otis and the MG's. That we were included in that was also something of a phenomenon. That we were there? With those people? They were accepting us and that was one of the things that really moved Otis. He was happy to be included and it brought him a new audience. It was greatly expanded in Monterey."

Next in the set came the soul ballad I've Been Loving You Too Long (To Stop Now), with its surges of emotion, followed by a frantic revamp of The Rolling Stones' Satisfaction, possibly the one tune that all the crowd recognised. There was little respite before the closing standard Try A Little Tenderness, Redding's version building from a gentle, touching run through the verses to a pounding, orgasmic climax of sweaty, visceral, get-down urgency.

"I don't even remember who we followed at Monterey," says The Mar-Keys' (later Memphis Horns) trumpeter Wayne Jackson. "It didn't matter. When Otis went on stage it was all over. Whoever opened for us was finished. Otis took it over."

Monterey was a shop window like no other. In the wake of the January 1967 "Human Be-In" – a sizeable festival held in San Francisco's Golden Gate Park, which the major labels and much of the US media had missed out on – another hippy event was planned for six months later at the County Fairgrounds in the small town south of San Francisco on Monterey Bay. In those intervening months, the recording industry had woken up to the potential of West Coast rock. Jefferson Airplane, who'd released their first album, *Takes Off*, at the end of the previous year, had welcomed aboard new lead singer Grace Slick, and their single, Somebody To Love, was currently a big noise on Top 40 radio. The promoters also booked happening Los

Angeles bands The Byrds, The Mamas And The Papas and Buffalo Springfield, a new blues-rock-soul act known as The Electric Flag, plus British groups The Who and The Jimi Hendrix Experience. (It was to be the Experience's US live debut; few in the States knew the leader was an American exile.) The Indian sitar-player Ravi Shankar, virtuoso on an instrument espoused by an increasing number of rock groups, was an exotic addition.

Bearing in mind that Smokey Robinson, an executive of Berry Gordy's Tamla Motown stable of labels, was on the board of the Monterey festival, it seems peculiar that the "soul" contingent at the show was limited to just two artists: Lou Rawls, a rich-toned, sophisticated "establishment" singer, and Otis Redding.

"[Monterey] was another vista, another eye-opener, another historic moment," says Booker T. "Completely disregarding the concert, I was shocked and amazed because when we pulled into the town everything had changed from the conventional American city. Restaurants were giving away free food, the police were pretty much non-existent, nowhere to be found. People were letting other people sleep in their hotel rooms. It was an atmosphere that I had never experienced before. Hell's Angels were escorting us to the concert, it was a flip-flop."

A lot of acts "made it" in the wake of Monterey. CBS signed Big Brother & The Holding Company (featuring wannabe blues bellower Janis Joplin) for a huge advance, as well as The Electric Flag and Moby Grape. Warner Brothers, who already had The Grateful Dead, added The Jimi Hendrix Experience. Capitol gave big advances to Quicksilver Messenger Service and The Steve Miller Band, while Mercury, late to the ball, paid well over the odds for two Texas groups, Mother Earth and The Sir Douglas Quintet. But, Hendrix excepted, their performances at Monterey paled by comparison with that of the Prince of Southern soul. Here was yet another peak in the brief, scorching career of the great Georgia soul singer. He had scored his first hit in 1963 and, in each of the four subsequent years, he managed to scale a new summit. As Wayne Jackson recalled, Monterey transformed Redding from Stax's greatest star, who could trade R&B hits smash for smash with James Brown, to a genuine crossover artist who had huge appeal to the young white audience, the one which Berry Gordy's Motown singers so assiduously courted.

Redding, for so long spurned by white pop and rock DJs in the US, had finally broken through. Honed by almost a decade on the road working up from chitlin' circuit to clubs to ballroom and now to a rock festival, Otis was on the verge of greatness, preparing to make new music that would transcend barriers and explore new styles that would find him new audiences.

After Monterey, Otis took a rest. The strain his relentless style of singing had imposed on his voice throughout the preceding half-decade caused polyps – small tumour-like growths – to develop on the mucous membrane of his throat, and he needed an operation to remove them. After the operation he spent time recuperating at his "farm" – the 400-acre Big O Ranch just outside Macon, Georgia – and working on new material. One of the songs, (Sittin' On) The Dock Of The Bay, heralded the emergence of a new style for him, and seemed destined to capitalise on the breakthrough to the white audience he'd made at Monterey. Crossover on a grand scale was now inevitable.

2 Macon – *Home In Your Heart*

DAWSON, GEORGIA. A SMALL TOWN ON US Route 82, in cotton country and sharecropping land about 100 miles south of Macon. Otis Redding Senior was a minister of a local church and, with his wife Fannie, had six children, four girls and two boys. The eldest son, Otis Redding Junior was born on September 9, 1941.

Three years later, the Redding family moved to an apartment in the Tindall Heights Housing Project in Macon. Lacking the studied gentility, separateness and submerged craziness of Savannah (see John Berendt's Midnight In The Garden Of Good And Evil) or the millennial dynamism of Atlanta, Macon was a Southern city awaiting rebirth. It has since remembered one of its favourite sons in a series of place names (the Otis Redding Bridge, formerly the Fifth Street Bridge, is the most obvious); for what Clarksdale, Mississippi and Dockery's Plantation have come to mean to Delta blues, Macon, Georgia is to soul. Little Richard, James Brown, Otis Redding – three men who fundamentally shaped African-American music in the '50s, '60s, '70s and beyond – all started their careers here, Brown and Redding beginning as Little Richard-style rock'n'roll shouters. (Coincidentally, for a while all three became synonymous with their signature shouts – Richard Penniman's "A-wop-bop-a-loo-bop-awop-bam-boom", Brown's assortment of grunts, "hit me's" and other imprecations to his band, and Redding's "gotta gotta".)

Initially, Otis Redding Sr worked at the Robbins Air Force Base – where James Brown had tap-danced by the railroad tracks for the entertainment of troops being moved in and out of the base – and preached on the weekends. But soon after arriving in Macon, he was laid low by tuberculosis and for long periods was unable to work. Fannie, Otis Jr, younger brother Rodgers and the four sisters coped with the hard times which an unreliable income brought, and moved out of the Tindall Heights into a small wooden house in the less salubrious Bellevue in west Macon, known to the locals as "Hellview". The Reddings did not last long there – the house burned down and they moved back to the Tindall Heights.

Otis Jr attended the Ballard-Hudson Senior High until the tenth grade, but then finances got tighter and he dropped out to help feed the family. He worked drilling wells at $1.25 an hour and then as a gas station attendant. Music was already playing a big role in his life; but in this he was no different from the majority of Southerners. "My mother and father used to go to parties when I was a kid," he told Jim Delehant, then of Hit Parade magazine, in one of the last interviews he gave before his death. "We used to go out to a place called Sawyer's Lake in Macon. There was a calypso song out then called Run, Joe. My mother and daddy used to play that for me all the time. I just dug the groove. Ever since then I've been playing music."

He had started to play drums in school and, given Otis Sr's duties as a preacher, was a regular in the gospel choir. As a teenager in Macon, Otis had musical competition from two quarters – Little Willie Jones, as his name might suggest a big fan of Little Willie John (a major early influence on James Brown), and Oscar Mack. Locals thought Mack and Jones had the voices to succeed in the big time and Mack, more obviously influenced by the attack of Little Richard, did cut a few sides with Stax. Penniman's influence was one that Redding happily conceded. "If it hadn't been for Little Richard I would not be here," he admitted in 1965. "I entered the music business because of Richard – he is my inspiration. I used to sing like Little Richard, his rock'n'roll stuff, you know. Richard has soul, too. My present music has a lot of him in it. He did a number way back called Directly From My Heart To You, which was the personification of soul, and he had one out – I heard it in LA a lot – called I Don't Know What You've Got But It's Got Me. Yes, sir. Little Richard has done a lot for me and my soul brothers in the music business."

Jones, Redding and a bass singer named Eddie Ross sang doo wop on the streets in the early evening, and every Sunday morning Otis sat behind a rudimentary kit and played drums for the gospel acts that entertained folks on DJ Hamp Swain's show on WIBB, the local radio station. He earned six dollars a show.

When Otis had his tonsils removed – a very fashionable operation in the '50s, they went along with the adenoids – he was deeply concerned about the effect it would have on his voice, and whether indeed he'd ever be able to sing again. Rodgers Redding recalls Otis Sr reassuring Jr. "My father said, 'Sure. Probably you be able to sing better.'"

In the eighth grade, Otis had started to expand his repertoire of instruments and picked up some basic piano and guitar skills, which allowed him to try to write his own songs. He never grew to be sophisticated on either instrument but managed well enough on open-tuned guitar.

Gladys Williams, a Macon pianist and bandleader, played regularly at the Hillview Springs Social Club. Kids weren't allowed to attend, but Otis would steal in, get at that piano and upstage the paid performers with his Little Richard thing. How they must have loved that. He soon began working with various Gladys Williams bands – an enterprising woman, she ran more than one at the same time – working the clubs in Bellevue and other Macon suburbs for $5–$10 a night.

Come 1958, Redding was able to test out his Richard

impersonation for real after Penniman, in October 1957, renounced rock'n'roll, declaring that he would enter theological college as a first step to ordination. With no Little Richard to all rootie the tutti frutti, and a lot of lucrative bookings to honour, James Brown was the first singer brought in to complete the star's itinerary on a big swing through the South. Later, with JB's star in the ascendant, Otis was hired. Like James, Otis had his Little Richard vocal licks down to a T, though Brown got a lot closer to the pompadour hairstyle. "Another young singer that we took on the road with us was Otis Redding," Henry Nash, Little Richard's long-time road manager and *compadre* remembered. "He idolised Richard. His impressions of Richard were word perfect and he had all of his moves down pat. He quit high school to come on the road with the Upsetters." Redding was able to mail home $25 a week, which at the time was a lifesaver to the struggling family.

His skill as a surrogate Little Richard had been sharpened by his singing in talent shows – particularly the Saturday morning Teenage Party live music radio shows, run by Hamp Swain at the Douglass Theatre in Macon. In the '50s, local DJs were important to any act anxious to get a career kickstarted. Swain had certainly been very helpful to the early career of James Brown. Like mandatory service in a gospel choir, success at a talent contest is a recurring signpost in the early years of many a soul star's career, and Redding conformed to the archetype by dominating the Teenage Party, winning for 15 consecutive weeks. On the sixteenth week, he was banned from entering. These successes were usually with covers of a Little Richard rock-'n'roller or a song made famous by Elvis Presley – like One Night, Money, Heebie Jeebies. "I remember it went, 'My bad luck baby put the jinx on me.' That song really inspired me to start singing," Otis told American author Stanley Booth. "I won the [Sunday night] talent show [at the Hillview Springs] for 15 straight nights with that song and then they wouldn't let me sing no more, wouldn't let me win that $5 any more."

All this success got his name known locally. Very known. After one show he met 15-year-old Zelma, his wife-to-be, whom he married in August 1961.

There, too, he met Johnny Jenkins. The regular, boyishly handsome features of Jenkins beam out from late '50s photographs of his band. He stands at the front, legs splayed at the start of the splits. Here's a cat who'll put on a rockin' good set, give the kids a show. Jenkins, allegedly an influence on Jimi Hendrix, was also once part of a Little Richard band, but now was too far along in his career to contest the talent shows at the Douglass Theatre. But he saw Rockhouse Redding, the big man so clearly inspired by Macon's greatest star, and thought Otis's band left something to be desired. He offered his services. "Well, he sounded great with me playing behind him – and he knowed it," Jenkins once said. "The first gig we played, we play at this little lounge. I say, 'How much you pay me?' He say, '25 cents.' I say, 'Well, that be all right, maybe you better pay me 15 cents now, 10 cents at the gig.'" A nice story but Jenkins was the man with the band, The Pinetoppers, and the bookings, via Phil Walden.

Walden, a white kid in love with R&B and rock-'n'roll, was only a year older than Otis. Like his younger brother Alan, he'd been turned on to R&B by the eldest Walden brother, Clark. As fraternity president at the Sidney Lanier High School, Phil got the chance to book bands – he chose the convenient theme of Rock'n'roll Party. And now here he was, sitting in his car outside the segregated

Douglass Theatre listening to a group he managed, The Heartbreakers, getting torched yet again by this guy named Redding.

On another occasion, Phil Walden hired a group with the sort of name that screamed identity crisis – Pat T. Cake And The Mighty Panthers. The guitar player was Johnny Jenkins; the singer was Little Willie Jones. Not long after, he heard that Jenkins had left Pat T. Cake to bake him a band of his own and Walden went to see the newly formed Pinetoppers at Lakeside Amusement Park. During a break between shows, he was introduced to Redding. He remembered the singer who'd burned his band at many a Douglass Theatre contest.

By now, Walden had left high school and was studying at Mercer University, Macon. He was still booking bands and hired The Pinetoppers; the act was based around Jenkins's flamboyant way with a guitar. Otis was featured singing Little Richard covers and pop hits like There Goes My Baby and Endlessly. They also did a very passable impersonation of the Clyde McPhatter-period Drifters, Money Honey being the original of choice.

In the summer of 1960, Redding headed west on his

own to Los Angeles to try his luck with the more thriving recording scene there. Staying with one of his sisters in California, he worked at a car wash to pay for his keep and cut four sides which were leased to Finer Arts (She's Alright, based on Barrett Strong's Money, and Tuff Enough as Otis And The Shooters) and Alshire (I'm Gettin' Hip/ Gamma Lamma). They were met with a stultifying lack of enthusiasm and he soon returned to Macon and Johnny Jenkins's Pinetoppers.

When local promoter-manager Bobby Smith booked a Battle Of The Bands show into the Lakeside Park, Jenkins, Otis and The Pinetoppers won it with a particularly wild and crazy performance. Smith – later better known as the manager of Wayne Cochran, a white-haired, blue-eyed soulman who favoured a vast horn section – recorded Otis for his inflammatorily named Confederate label. The songs, Shout Bamalama and Fat Girl, offered yet more Little Richard cloning – it was something that needed to be worked out of the system. Cochran was on bass for the sessions at the Athens, Georgia studio. Shout Bamalama, nearly but not quite a verse left out of Gamma Lamma, was plugged to extinction by the loyal and indefatigable Hamp Swain (WIBB) and John R (WLAC) in the summer of 1961. (Although Shout Bamalama found no commercial success at the time, it became a Number 11 R&B hit in the US for one Mickey Murray in the very month of Otis's death in 1967, on Shelby Singleton's SSS International label.)

That summer of 1961, Otis married Zelma. "He was determined to just go out and mess around with musicians every day and say, 'I'm gonna get a hit record, I'm gonna be a star,'" Zelma told writer Pete Guralnick. "And everything he told me, I just believed him, because he believed in himself to the fullest. I've never seen his weakness; I guess that's what made me strong. He was very positive about himself and his music." Buoyed up by Zelma's love, faith and confidence in him, he devoted himself to music. She got a job.

Meanwhile, the brash young Mr Walden had formed Phil Walden & Associates – a very grand name to make a one-man operation sound big – who could be found at the Professional Building [later Robert E. Lee] on Mulberry Street, the same block of offices that was home to the WIBB radio station and Bobby Smith. Walden, who was still in college, hired out permutations of The Pinetoppers' line-up depending on the size of the venue and the fee promised. Inevitably, in the hurly-burly of uncertain cash flow which is the hallmark of the entertainment business, the hard-pressed student Walden got into a fine financial pickle and found no relief when he applied to his father for help. Upon discovering his young friend's plight, Redding went into the neighbourhood and begged and borrowed the money from friends and acquaintances. "You do the learning, I got to do the singing," he said.

Succour of a more permanent nature was at hand – Johnny Jenkins had a local hit with Love Twist. In Atlanta's financial centre there lived and worked a banker named James Newton who thought he would make Johnny Jenkins a star and himself some money by recording a guitar instrumental for his hobby label, Tifco. (It is strange how Southern bankers, presumably bored, started record labels – a recurring theme in this story.) So Jenkins and The Pinetoppers cut the energetic Love Twist backed with Pinetop, which was plugged on Macon radio by local DJ Frank Clark. Joe Galkin, a well-known promotion man in the South for Atlantic, heard it and leased it for his own label, Gerald. It sold another 25,000 before Galkin gave it to Atlantic for distribution in September 1961. (Atlantic, started in 1946, had grown to become one of the largest independents in the country and would reach new heights with its imminent association with soul.)

By now, Walden had graduated from Mercer. After the local success of Love Twist, the manager pushed for another recording date for Jenkins and The Pinetoppers; Galkin persuaded Atlantic to finance the session. Walden insisted that both Jenkins and Redding be recorded, despite Galkin's reservations (he thought Shout Bamalama "the worst record I ever heard. I told Phil, he's a lousy singer"). Nonetheless, The Pinetoppers session was set up. The venue was to be the Stax Studios in Memphis. It meant quite a drive from Macon, but Atlantic had a distribution deal with Jim Stewart's young label and had been impressed by the studio band, Booker T. And The MG's, which was enjoying its first national hit with a simple yet sophisticated evergreen called Green Onions.

3 Memphis – *Soul Stew*

THE MOST FAMOUS MUSIC THOROUGHFARE in Memphis, Tennessee, Beale Street is actually little more than three or four blocks of one- and two-storey buildings. Despite a name beaming with musical heritage, there is a feeling that – apart from the private enterprises of Elvis Presley's Graceland and the famed Sun Records studio on Union Avenue – Beale Street and the rest of the city has been losing out in investment to the rich, white metropolis of Nashville. In fact, Memphis itself has seemed somehow dismissive of, or ashamed by, its rich musical heritage, as though this is a disreputable relative one would like to ignore or be rid of, no matter that the world outside attaches considerable importance to its role in 20th-century history. Nowhere is this attitude more vividly illustrated than at the junction of East McLemore Avenue and College Road. It's a mile away from the sumptuous Peabody Hotel, in whose umbra squats Beale Street, but 10,000 miles distant in terms of wealth. This corner lot was once the site of a grocery store, a movie house and an electrical goods store. Then it became home to Stax Records, the best Southern soul studio and label in the '60s and early '70s, when it was a hive of recording activity and a consistent supplier of pop, soul and R&B hits.

After its demise there were several attempts to establish a Stax Museum. A small corner in the huge Memphis Pyramid, then being built on the banks of the Mississippi at a cost of $65 million, once seemed to offer a suitable location, but somewhere along the way the idea was lost and you had to go to The Memphis Music Hall Of Fame to get a historical reconstruction of the label and a perspective on its heyday. Obviously, a building on the original site would have been ideal but in the '80s the Church Of God In Christ acquired the then redundant Stax Studios and started to demolish the building. They were about a third of the way through their work before the city burghers woke up to the fact that a site of historic interest was being razed to the ground and gained an injunction to stop the work. It was just a reprieve, as it turned out, not a halt, and the Church duly completed its work.

On a cold early evening in February 1996, a few hours before sundown, Wayne Jackson stands on the corner of McLemore and College and eyes a six-foot-high metal pole cemented in the middle of the sidewalk. There are many such poles planted around Memphis and the plaques they hold aloft commemorate local achievements. This particular sign, the least well kept in the city, is bent and defaced with paint. It reads: "On this site stood Stax Records Incorporated, which boasted such stars as Otis Redding, Rufus and Carla Thomas, Isaac Hayes, The Staple [sic] Singers, Albert King, The Bar-Kays . . ."

The coarse grass covering the derelict site is flattened and worn. No weeds grow here. Cars and trucks steadily stream by on McLemore as Jackson attempts to kick free an old brick embedded in the hard earth.

"Here's a brick! One they missed! [Tourists] will still pay about $15 for it."

A path has been trodden diagonally across the barren lot where the Capitol Theatre's cinema seats, and then recording desks, microphones and instruments, once stood.

"We'll stand where Otis stood," Jackson says, searching for his bearings on the lot. "This is Otis's spot."

He is standing on a small rise of earth two thirds of the way back from McLemore (it is pronounced "Mackel-moore" locally).

"On the corner of College and McLemore this was one long building, kinda like a little plaza. Jack's Number Two was a grocery store on the very corner." A slab of the concrete flooring which belonged to Jack's grocery store is still there. "Then, next to Jack's Number Two, the Capitol Theatre began. It had two sets of swinging doors. The ticket booth's in the middle and on either side of that was a pair of swinging doors that you walked through. The right-hand swinging doors went into where the popcorn stand was – it became Miss Axton's record shop. She called it The Satellite Records Studio Shop. The left-hand doors went into the studio. You'd go down to where you'd go to the bathrooms. The bathrooms were the echo chamber. And then you'd go through the theatre door into the back where the slanted floor went down. And that was where we'd taken the chairs out and put the microphones up."

Behind the façade, the Capitol took up most of the lot. "Next to the Capitol Theatre was an electronics place, they fixed televisions and stuff. And then the other side of that was Slim Jenkins's Joint, which was an old greasy hamburger place. And then, of course, eventually Stax bought everything. First thing they did was buy the electronics place and make that into East Publishing. Then they bought Slim Jenkins's Joint and extended the offices into that. Then they bought Jack's Number Two and the next thing you know this whole area was Stax Records."

It became as strong an attraction to the local population as any film at the Capitol had been. "The Mad Lads had their shoeshine stand right in front of Jack's Number Two. And they would shine our shoes – they were little boys then – and sing and do dance steps out here to try to get us to put them on a record. And that went on until they finally got a record that was a hit record. That's the way it was – the shoeshine boys out front, we took 'em in. If you had nerve enough to walk in the studio and say, 'I wanna be a singer', in two more hours you might be the singer. And that was true of Sun Records. If you had the nerve you could get something done. David Porter worked at that grocery store [he points across the street to a long, flat, dirty white building with a laundry annexe] and he'd come over here with a song, every day. 'I got me a song, I got me a song.'" Finally, Porter became the first Stax songwriter on staff.

As a business, Stax Records had its beginnings in the mid-'50s with 25-year-old country music fan Jim Stewart, who was working at the First Tennessee bank and playing fiddle in a country band. When he felt and heard the waves the Memphis recordings of Elvis Presley were making – Stewart's country band and Presley very occasionally shared the same bill locally – he thought he too would get something down on record, a procedure about which he knew nothing. He did not care much for R&B in the beginning – and possibly never did – but as a bank employee he could read a balance sheet. Jim's sister, Estelle Axton, a teller at the Union Planters Bank, mortgaged her house, which allowed Stewart to buy an Ampex recorder. Her son, Charles "Packy" Axton, a wild child by every account, played saxophone and did not consider country music to be as prime rib as did his uncle. He convinced a school friend at Messick that his basic guitars, bass and drums band needed horns. The friend was guitarist Steve Cropper and the band was The Royal Spades, who were completed by bassist Donald "Duck" Dunn, drummer Terry Johnson and guitarist Charlie Freeman, acknowledged by many as the best young player in Memphis at the time. The Spades didn't want horns, however. Eventually, they changed their name to The Marquis, which few could pronounce, so they phoneticised it to become The Mar-Keys.

When Axton let slip that his uncle and mother had a recording studio, Cropper thought that maybe his band perhaps could use horns after all. The studio was, in fact, a storehouse in Brunswick, Tennessee which became the band's rehearsal room. They were not complete greenhorns. Cropper's instrumental Flea Circus was recorded by Bill Justis in 1958, when the guitarist was just 15, and he had done a few sessions at Sam Phillips's studio, notably with Jerry Lee Lewis. Wayne Jackson, the last piece in the Mar-Keys jigsaw, was an experienced trumpeter with a CV that ran from rock'n'roll to the Arkansas All State Symphony.

"And do you know," Jackson laughs, "ever since then I'm always waiting for someone to tap me on the shoulder and tell me, 'It's over, the adventure's over, time to go back to Arkansas.'"

Jim Stewart eventually gave up his dream of turning a Tennessee warehouse into a recording studio and leased a more suitable facility, a disused movie house, the Capitol Theatre, at 926 East McLemore Avenue. Rufus Thomas and his daughter Carla were the first acts recorded there and their Cause I Love You, a charmingly innocent pop-R&B sound, kicked up a fuss for Satellite Records. After three years and eight releases, the label was at last making ripples well outside the mid-South. It soon became a magnet for local talent – virtually all African-American – as well as a lure to bigger fish. Atlantic Records executive Jerry Wexler agreed to pick up Cause I Love You and all future (Rufus and Carla) Thomas records, as well as securing first refusal on distribution of all future releases on the label.

Estelle Axton's Record Shop at the front of the studios became a focal point for wannabes and also for testing the popularity of the label's latest products. Up in

Detroit, Berry Gordy's Motown had its committee of artists and staff who judged how well a new production had turned out; Satellite used the kids on the Memphis streets.

Carla Thomas had cut a second song at Satellite, Gee Whizz, which she'd written two years earlier when she was 16. "Do not confuse this with any other record on any other label!" screamed the trade press ads that Atlantic took out to plug the record, lest store owners confuse the song with The Innocents' recording of the same name. Listeners did not and Carla's Whizz reached Number 5 on the R&B charts and Number 10 on the national pop charts. But perhaps the fundamental sound that defined all the music that would come out of the Capitol building in the next eight years was an instrumental recorded, apparently, over a period of months by a huge amalgam of musicians at a variety of sessions. Begun back in the Brunswick warehouse and Satellite's last hit record, The Mar-Keys' Last Night was a honking, stonking dance record, driven by a barking, braying horn section, a beefy drum sound, edgily energetic organ and piano. It was suggestive of waking up still wired from the joys of the dance and frolics the night before, when youth and energy meant you had no hangover. Baritone saxophonist Floyd Newman growled "Oooh, last night!" with unequivocal lubricity.

It was a sound that reeked of the city after dark. "Memphis in the '60s was a wild town," says Wayne Jackson. "There were rhythm and blues bands everywhere, there were black guys in mohair suits doin' all that shit and we were doin' it with them. We were white guys, The Mar-Keys were all white until we got into Stax and got a black drummer, a black keyboard player and a black horn player. Nobody even thought about that. Integration was not a topic because we didn't think about it because we were just young people and we were working together in the studio, recording music, and they were paying us a little, we didn't have to have a job and we were always the same. Me and [saxophonist] Andrew [Love] worked hard not to have a job. And never had one. And here we are at 50 wondering how long I can keep on not havin' a job!"

Atlantic picked up Last Night for national distribution but by now another, longer established label in California also called Satellite insisted on having the name. So the Memphis label's owners took the first two letters of the founder/owners' surnames – Stewart and Axton – and renamed their company Stax. Chips Moman, who had been a session musician, writer and producer in the early years of the label, fell out with Stewart and Stax soon after, and Cropper was brought in as staff writer/producer and session guitarist.

"He was the first to leave The Mar-Keys and go to work here in the studio for Jim Stewart," Jackson said. "He became Jim Stewart's studio guy. Jim needed somebody like that who knew a little bit about rhythm and blues because Jim was a country man, he liked country music. He hated me and Andrew, he hated horns, he didn't understand them. He liked fiddles. Truly, he was a country fiddle player, that's what he was. And all of a sudden he found himself in the rhythm and blues music business and it had to be a shock to him. So he got Steve Cropper out of our band, a young white guy who understood rhythm and blues, to come into the studio and be a studio guy and promised him a part of the action. That's why Steve was always writing with Otis, writing with Wilson Pickett, writing, writing with everybody and sharing in writer's royalties. That was his deal with Jim."

Cropper deserved it, too. By now, his simple yet

inimitable style as a rhythm guitarist was well on the way to full maturity. "Flash don't make cash," was his guitar credo. "I find a hole and and complement what everyone else is doing, and leave a hole or two in the process." As individual musicians, the MG's were all like that – excellent accompanists who listened to the song and kept their contributions succinct and to the point. Throughout the '60s, Cropper's solos were models of drive, energy and marvellous economy; in the second half of the decade, as many a Hendrix-inspired "axeman" became overheated, his Fender Telecaster made the unanswerable case for understatement.

New singers, musicians and writers arrived at Stax in a flow as steady as the wide Mississippi's. David Porter came and wrote his first Stax song with Marvell Thomas, Rufus's keyboard-playing son, for Barbara Stephens. William Bell had been brought to the label by Chips Moman, and straight off the bat he wrote and recorded You Don't Miss Your Water, a ballad that perfectly mixed the pain of blues and grandeur of gospel to conjure pure Southern soul. It had quickly become apparent that to better complement the work of the singers and writers, musicians of higher calibre had to be used. They were not hard to find in Memphis. Individuals from trumpeter Willie Mitchell's band, a local quintet that had a reputation for being the city's best, most versatile and seasoned players, were hired for sessions – notably bassist Lewis Steinberg, who had played on one of the versions of Last Night, and drummer Al Jackson Jr.

A very young baritone saxophonist, Booker T. Jones, turned out to be a precocious multi-instrumentalist and, between classes, became a fixture in the studios on organ or piano. "I started playing in clubs when I was barely in the ninth grade, I was 14 years old. My father would take me or have another adult take me and bring me home. I started playing bass and baritone sax with Willie Mitchell. That was my first gig, baritone sax. Al Jackson was in the band, Lewis Steinberg was on bass. It was a blues band but we played some jazz tunes also."

Jones followed Steinberg, Jackson and The Mar-Keys to Stax. His first MG's session was Green Onions. "We had played before, but not as Booker T. And The MG's. We had played just as a group of people working together for sessions. We played as The Triumphs, but never as Booker T. It was supposed to be a Billy Lee Riley session but I don't remember him turning up that day. I just remember having free time and Green Onions being the song recorded."

Later, Mar-Key Wayne Jackson, Floyd Newman and Andrew Love were hired and they developed the classic Stax horn sound. Wayne Jackson likens his meeting with Andrew Love to something akin to the spark between David Porter and Isaac Hayes. "We met and the magic happened. We had something. I met him in a nightclub, the Manhattan Club, where Willie Mitchell played. Andrew played with Willie Mitchell some and I'd go by there after my gigs and I would see this black guy and when he'd play his saxophone everybody stopped and looked at him, and I knew he had something special going on."

And so for recording purposes, the personnel became two groups – The Mar-Keys and, without the horn section, Booker T. And The MG's, whose first single from that aborted Billy Lee Riley session, Green Onions, shot to Number 1 on the R&B charts and reached Number 3 pop, establishing the label's credentials as an operation with a distinctive sound and flavour. Jones, who had sung gospel in church from an early age and "a little bit in the clubs", had wanted to sing more with the band, but "the idea at

Stax was to keep Booker T. And The MG's instrumental, because of the success, and to keep them as a backing band. The success as an instrumental group was accepted but it wasn't accepted with the same enthusiasm, I don't think, as the success by other vocal artists. So there were some stumbling blocks there because we wore so many hats and played so many roles – songwriters, arrangers, back-up band, producers."

In fact, the MG's and the Stax set-up "was a family. We knew each other's personal lives, we ate together, we had lunch and very often had dinner together, ate at each other's homes. It really was a family. A big family. People were coming and going so we knew each other very well.

"Back on the McLemore lot, I go to throw away the half-brick I had dug up. 'Oh no I want that! This could be worth a lot of money! Solid gold!' Jackson tosses it up and catches it a couple of times. 'The sun's still up so we can stay . . . for a few minutes. When the sun goes down, we're gettin' out.'"

4 McLemore Magic

THE SUCCESS OF LAST NIGHT AND GREEN Onions alerted Stax to the potential inherent in instrumental hits. Bill Black's Combo, the bassist-led instrumental group who were based in Memphis and recording for Willie Mitchell's nearby Hi label, had enjoyed five Top 20 US pop hits in 1960 alone. So when Atlantic promotion man Joe Galkin recommended that Stax should record Johnny Jenkins, the front man on the local instrumental hit Love Twist, the studio readily agreed to a session. Otis Redding drove the rented station wagon from Macon to Memphis with Jenkins, which led to some early press misunderstanding that he was no more than the guitarist's roadie or chauffeur. However, when Jenkins's session turned into something of a disaster, Galkin and Phil Walden urged that the three-hour session be completed usefully by cutting the new singer. In the final 40 minutes, Otis recorded two tracks. (In fact his manager, Walden, had prepared Redding and Galkin for this opportunity because of his doubts about Jenkins's star potential; but the Stax session supervisor, Jim Stewart, and the studio musicians were not expecting another artist on the session.)

Stewart's agreement was smoothed after he was promised 50 per cent of the publishing on anything released. Johnny Jenkins played guitar, Lewis Steinberg bass and Al Jackson Jr drums; who played keyboards is open to debate. Some accounts, including that of the reliable Rob Bowman, author of innumerable sleevenotes, booklets and an essential history of Stax, Soulsville, say Booker T. had already left, so Cropper played piano. But Jones told me: "The first time we worked together was in the studio doing a demo with him for Jim Stewart on These Arms Of Mine. I was playing piano or organ. His sincerity and dedication to the moment was so emotional and that's what he put into every effort. The times I spent with Otis were moving, the musical time and the friendship time was the same."

In the studio, they sped through a happy-go-lucky Hey Hey Baby, a perfunctory, ingenuous Little Richard impersonation. In the time left, the singer and band cut a ballad – fast-slow was the habitual A-side/B-side division of styles on a single – written by Redding, called These Arms Of Mine, a blueprint for future Otis ballads. The one usable sound from the session, it was released on Stax's Volt subsidiary and Stewart assigned his share of the publishing to John Richbourg of Nashville's powerful WLAC radio station. This sensible and not uncommon move ensured that from its release in October 1962 the record got steady coverage on John R's show, a dripfeed of exposure which ensured that the single inexorably had crept up the R&B charts by March 1963. It peaked at 20 and crossed over to hit 85 on the pop charts.

Although clearly not yet the finished article as a singer, the Otis Redding on These Arms Of Mine has many of the vocal signatures for which he'd become known in the next few years and which would be widely copied. But it is the earthy tone and his determined pleading that makes every syllable resonate with honesty. He gave full vent to Georgia pronunciations – "liddle" for "little", "bl-yew" for "blue" and others, most of which became identifiable Reddingisms. The song itself is a steadily paced country ballad and he states his case with genuine feeling. The piano, the steady tread of Steinberg and Jackson and Jenkins's more flowery guitar wrap Redding's simple, moving reading in soul-country beauty.

He went on the road to promote it with a band that included blues guitarist Eddie Kirkland, a graduate of the John Lee Hooker band, Macon friend Oscar Mack and, from New Orleans, Bobby Marchan, all of whom Stax recorded. (Jenkins and The Pinetoppers went back on the road playing club and college campus dates. He remained a solid live draw on the circuit until 1969, when Atlantic recorded *Ton Ton Macoute*, an album which sold poorly.)

Stax's senior partners were in no hurry to record a follow-up session – Stewart had not been all that enamoured of These Arms. But in June 1963, the singer was called back to Memphis to cut another ballad. That's What My Heart Needs has similar roots to These Arms – they're both country-soul ballads – though the piano triplets of the first were replaced with chords picked out by Cropper's guitar and Al Jackson Jr's ticking off 16 beats to the bar on the hi-hat. When Wayne Jackson's trumpet figure enters after the first verse, the long and crucial relationship between Otis and the Stax horn section begins. The balance between country and soul quickly swings to the latter after only one verse as Otis, audibly brimming with confidence in the studio, takes control of the song. His arms are empty again but there's a grittier reason – he's lost that woman to another man. The plea for her to return is all the more forlorn and passionate as he builds to the stripped-bare emotion of the final verse, the first example of Otis Redding's aggressive, heartfelt testifying. The flip side, Mary's Little Lamb, sets the nursery rhyme to an R&B arrangement pitched somewhere near Rufus Thomas's Walkin' The Dog. It was the only track released in Otis's lifetime that used background vocals as well as a horn section, but the voice "baa-ing" deep in the mix is an ovine jest too far.

Although That's What My Heart Needs offered further proof of Redding's potential, this more tortured performance commercially fared less well than These

Arms Of Mine, and was his worst-selling Volt single while he was alive. Otis's third single, Pain In My Heart, did better. 'Adapted' from Ruler Of My Heart a little too closely for the liking of its composer Allen Toussaint, who had written it originally for Irma Thomas and published it under the pseudonym Naomi Neville (Toussaint's mum), Pain In My Heart was originally credited as a Redding composition. Legal representations from Toussaint quickly stopped that piece of subterfuge. Redding's interpretation, recorded almost a full year after his first Stax session, is another matter. No copyright problem here: his tone, phrasing and attack are Georgia, not Louisiana. "Otis was a real genius," Wayne Jackson pondered. "He had all the songs in his head when he came into the studio. He had most of the horn lines, the whole song. Bass line, guitar, everything. We learned a lot from him. Otis didn't know any music outside of what he could hum you. He played bar chords on the guitar, tuned to open E, played bar chords with his index finger and he'd strum on it and move up and down the neck but he couldn't even make a C chord. So he would really just thump the guitar and sing his words and hum the horn lines and pat out the drum thing, he was really intuitive, he was just born that way."

Any hint of country in his voice has been leached out on Pain In My Heart; the mixture is blues, gospel and soul ballad. The horns participate from the start, braying a mournful refrain. Cropper's guitar carries on a running commentary whether laying out chords or riffing, and Jackson's excitedly ticking hi-hat again beats 16 against the steadier four/four of the snare and bass drums. The modulated swell of horns in the middle-eight forms a framework arrangement that many Stax soul ballads would follow.

The B-side of Pain In My Heart was a bona fide Redding original, co-written with Phil Walden, titled Something Is Worrying Me. Paced at a crisp, mid-tempo with Booker T's extraordinarily busy piano rippling in the background, the song is dominated by Redding (naturally), and the interplay between the horn section and Al Jackson's drumming. It's the first Redding track in which the colours of the horn section play such a prominent role. "We did define [the Southern soul horn style] but we didn't know what we were doing," Wayne Jackson explained. "We were not even experimenting, we were just playing what we could play. Simple stuff."

Horn lines were rudimentary and instinctive. "There wasn't a whole lot to do to them, all we had to do was just straighten them out," added Jackson. "If you'll notice on all of those records a lot of that stuff is unison, playing all the same notes. But we could hear simple harmonies same way he could. He usually had his lyrics together when he got there. He and Steve [Cropper] wrote the songs together and a lot of times I would write with them and do the horn lines while they would write the songs. When we recorded, he would sing because he didn't have a track to come back to later. So regardless of if he didn't have the song ready when he got there when we recorded that was what went down. Whatever he did – whether it was 'Hmm, Hmm, Hmm' or 'Oh baby, oh baby' or 'gotta, gotta, gotta' – that's what was on the record. So the equipment defined it, the equipment spoke to that. And so if I made a mistake I'd say, 'Oh wait a minute', and I made mistakes on a lot of those records that I would have liked to have changed, done again . . . and almost inevitably if I made a mistake that was the cut they wanted to keep. I would say, 'Can we do it again?' and Otis or Jim Stewart would say, 'That one felt great! Let's use it!'"

Redding's first album, *Pain In My Heart*, was released on January 1, 1964. With two hits – small on a national scale but very strong in certain territories – and a real buzz about him from anyone who'd seen him, there was reason for confidence. As well as the first two A-sides and Hey Hey Baby, the album had versions of Stax hits (Rufus Thomas's The Dog, the first in the Memphis stalwart's kennel of canine dance songs), songs by his two major influences (Sam Cooke's You Send Me and Little Richard's Lucille) and contemporary hits without which no touring artist would be able to strike up a band (Richard Berry's ubiquitous Louie, Louie, Ben E. King's Stand By Me and the Don Gardner/Dee Dee Ford hit I Need Your Lovin').

Another track off *Pain In My Heart* was the Otis original Security, which later became his fifth single, released in April 1964 and reaching 97 on the pop charts (Billboard's R&B charts had been suspended for 14 months from November 1963). Otis's plea for emotional Security is announced by a trumpet/sax fanfare and settles into a mid-tempo groove with Cropper's chopped chords and rich-toned riffing and Al Jackson's drumming prompting from just behind the beat. Duck Dunn's bass line (he had taken over from Lewis Steinberg, who was less in tune with the Stax direction) is a thing of busy and flexible beauty.

"When I graduated, Otis Redding had a song called Security and I thought that was one of the greatest songs I ever heard in my life," Southern soul balladeer Percy Sledge remembers. "I used to shoot eight ball behind that song until these guys unplugged the Rock-Ola, 'cos I played it over and over and over again. You know when you shoot pool you always talkin' trash, disturbin' the other guy that you're shootin' at. The one with the biggest mouth was always the one that was winnin'. (Laughs) And Security was one of my good pool songs. I never got tired of hearing that. Send somebody to keep puttin' quarters in, the same song over and over again. The people that was sittin' around, they loved the song theyselves. But the guys that were shootin' pool would be yellin', 'Unplug that thing!'

"Otis was the backbone of the whole thing. To meet him, that's how I really got to meet Phil Walden. [Walden became Sledge's manager and he later recorded for Walden's Capricorn label.] Otis was tops. I think I was at senior high school when I first heard Otis Redding. He was my Number 1 man as far as soul music was concerned in my lifetime, down those days. Him and Joe Tex, 'cos I always have admired good singers. "

Perhaps the most remarkable aspect about the *Pain In My Heart* tracks, especially the Redding originals, is the speed at which the Stax style is coalescing around his voice. His enthusiasm had clearly infected the studio musicians: they're trying things and playing with a certainty and confidence that's borne of his faith in them and the fun that they're so obviously having. "He was magical from the beginning," Wayne Jackson recalled, "his personality was so magnetic. He exuded happiness, he was a happy man. He was havin' a good time and he was climbin' to the top and he took us with him. Fast ride, too."

The single that preceded Security (Otis's fourth) was Come To Me, released in February 1964. This was a gentler, beseeching soul ballad, a rarity in that it has no horns and a piano plinking eight notes to the bar. Co-written with Phil Walden, the lyric uses a "these arms of mine" phrase to jog the listener's mind that this was indeed Otis Redding. The choke in his voice does not sound too convincing. Its flip side, Don't Leave Me This Way, sung with all stops out, is another Redding-Walden collaboration, probably written on tour in a shared motel room. It never appeared on an album in his lifetime and has surfaced on only a few collections since his death, notably the first volume of three 6-CD box sets cataloguing the *Complete Stax/Volt Soul Singles* and a deleted Charly LP. Come To Me, however, was included on his second album, *The Great Otis Redding Songs Soul Ballads*, released in March 1965.

By that time, Booker T. Jones had left high school – and Stax. "I went to Indiana University so I could learn more [about music] and I think what I learned and brought back was good for Stax. I had started at Indiana in '62 and I was a senior in '66 and I had to do one more course to get my degree at Memphis State in '67. So I was the one who studied. There were some knowledgeable musicians, all the horn players read, so I was able to converse with them. And the string players from Memphis, they all read so I was able to write for them, but I was the only one in the rhythm section that went to high school and college for music. It was a double-edged sword. It gave me a little more responsibility in the group because I was a member of the family and the only one able to put it down on paper, so I had the added responsibility of doing the lead sheets. For a while in addition to doing my homework I would have to leave the sessions and I would have to go home and write the lead sheets of the songs for that day. And I would have to converse with the band about the key and arrangements. However, that worked to my advantage also because it helped me solidify my position there and gave me a little more control over the music, over the arrangements and so forth."

His absence gave a chance to another young keyboard player who for years had been trying to get a break at the studio.

"I had had three auditions with Stax," Isaac Hayes recalls. "One was with Calvin Valentine & Swing Cats, I was the vocalist. One was with a group called The Ambassadors, they was like a doo wop group, and another was a group called The Teen Tones, another doo wop group I sang with. I sang bass with those groups. And we was turned down each time. I mean, everybody wanted to be at Stax, especially all the blacks who lived in Memphis at that time because Stax was happening with Rufus and Carla, Rufus doin' The Dog and Booker T. And The MG's with Green Onions and The Mar-Keys with Last Night, they were just having some successes. And everybody wanted to be there."

Eventually, while working as a keyboard player with the band of Floyd Newman, who was also a Stax staff reed player, almost exclusively baritone sax, Hayes got the call. "And when I got there, Jim Stewart offered me a staff position as one of the musicians. I was thrilled to death. [Booker T.] was off at Indiana University and they needed a keyboard player. They had a guy named Joe Hall, who played on a lot of Willie Mitchell's stuff, and they also chose me. They kinda threw me in the fire.

"The first session was an Otis Redding album session. I would have been around 21 or 22, and Otis, when I first saw him, he was a tall guy, a statue of a man. He had a natural hair style, those were just beginning to come in – Joe Tex and most guys were wearing the process. Maybe Otis in the earliest days with The Pinetoppers, he might have had it straightened, but when I saw him he had a natural. And he dressed well, silk mohair suit and a big grin on his face. Everybody knew him but me, of course, and I was a bit shy. He had Pain In My Heart, These Arms Of Mine.

"Everybody was gathering round and I went on down to the piano and I was introduced to him as the new keyboard player. He was very charismatic, he just lit up the environment wherever he was. Everybody was looking forward to it. Al Jackson then would tease him about sometimes the way he talked and some of his grammar but it didn't bother him at all. Yeah, he was country. Georgia. And he'd say [Isaac begins to stamp his feet], 'Yeah, Ah got this idea, 'bout this thing', seemed like he'd stomp a hole in the floor with his feet when he'd get started. Then he'd get hold of the guitar and start running the groove down, what he wanted, and everybody would kinda catch on to what he was doin'. And eventually we'd have a groove goin', then he'd have the horns come on – Wayne and Andrew and Gene ['Bowlegs' Miller], 'Daddle-daddle-daddle-dah-duh-laa!', running the horn lines down to 'em 'til they started workin' on that, and the next thing you know we'd pretty much have the arrangement in hand.

"Then everybody would go into their respective cubby holes, 'cos we only had a 1-track machine. Jim Stewart was called The King Of The One-Track. And Otis wouldn't have all of his lyrics down on a lot of them songs.

He was very spontaneous. And he would go back behind the mic, he could ad-lib his ass off. And the tune would kick off and sometimes we didn't have headsets but you could kinda hear him. He would be behind the mic just stompin', like he was marchin', and just making things up as he went along. We had our basic structure and he would work within the parameters of that structure. I mean, all these things he did.

"We'd run the cut, Jim Stewart would play it back, and we'd listen. He'd say, 'Well, y'all, we can do it again. We can do better than that.' Nowadays, when you do voice overs, you can take your time. You can do a line or two, dub it in, punch in, punch out. Back then, he had to sing it every time and if somebody screwed up everybody had to start all over again. But he attacked it with the same enthusiasm if it was the tenth take or the first take. He attacked it the same way."

Of course, he hardly ever needed 10 takes. "It was rare, but if we did it, he'd be right there, right on top of it."

The *Soul Ballads* album – which Hayes is sure he worked on though it fails to credit him – signalled another big leap forward for the singer, for Stax and for its house band and writers. First, Redding started writing with guitarist Steve Cropper, whose discipline, fast-growing knowledge of song structure and good instincts made him a perfect collaborator. Redding had no problem thinking up ideas for songs and grooves but would often be at a loss as to how best to organise and finish them. This was Cropper's forte. Secondly, the mantle of surrogate Little Richard was finally cast off as his cover versions now concentrated solely on slower tunes and he explored more fully the notion of walking in Sam Cooke's footsteps.

That's How Strong My Love Is, the track which opens the album, was brought in to Stax by Roosevelt Jamison, but despite Cropper's help the writer thought that the label had no interest in his song and recorded it with O.V. Wright at another Memphis label, Goldwax. However, Cropper had recorded it with Otis and the two were released at roughly the same time. Like many of Redding's ballad treatments, That's How Strong My Love Is has a very powerful rhythmic pulse, Cropper's guitar cementing Redding's lines in place. (Soon after its release The Rolling Stones covered the song. Indeed, most of Redding's A- and B-sides were now covered by R&B bands on the mushrooming soul scene in Britain.)

The versions of better-known songs on *Soul Ballads* vividly illustrate how Redding's idiosyncratic style and unique voice, in which Little Richard's uptempo attack and tone collide with Sam Cooke's phrasing, forged a distinctive new style like no other singer's of the time, and ensured that Otis could really make a song his own. The choice of material points to a liking for gospel-rooted ballad singers with a more sophisticated style than his own. Sam Cooke, possessor of a honeyed gospel tenor, who had become a suave swinger as comfortable on pop ditties as on standards with swinging, big band arrangements; Jackie Wilson, the versatile and very physical performer whose voice could soar with quasi-operatic splendour or who could sound just as at home on a jaunty, rock'n'roll novelty; and Jerry Butler, "The Ice Man" as he was known, who was as versatile as Wilson and Cooke but favoured the less fevered vocal approach, managing to suggest emotion without a lack of control, and mastered smoothness without seeming bland. The versatility and ease with a melody of all three meant that at various times their voices, at the behest of producers and/or record company, would be swathed in layers of violins, violas and cellos and the occasional heavenly choir.

This is something Redding never succumbed to. (Whether it would have been the inevitable conclusion had he continued in the new direction suggested by his last big hit is a matter of interesting conjecture.)

Otis's reading of Sam Cooke's 1962 hit Nothing Can Change This Love uses many of Cooke's idiosyncrasies without ever being close to mere imitation. Unlike his earliest Little Richard impersonations, this is Cooke filtered through Redding's experiences and emotions. The substantial difference in timbre of their voices – Otis's rawer edge is matched by the grit and sinew of the Stax house band's approach to the song – makes his variation on the theme into a very different song. His interpretation of Jackie Wilson's 1960 hit A Woman, A Lover, A Friend proceeds through a steady first verse and, encouraged by Cropper's background guitar, he lets out some slack during the second. In the broken arrangement of the chorus, he threatens to break free but never quite does so and, in the song's final passages, his flights into falsetto are unexpected and rare. For Your Precious Love, a 1958 pop and R&B hit, was virtually Jerry Butler's swan song with The Impressions (he quit two records later) and is a fine piece of remodelling as the purer, gospel-drenched Chicago soul is taken downhome by the Georgia-meets-Tennessee mid-South sensibilities of Redding and the Stax band. Cropper's country-soul guitar and the sympathetically muted horn section are given urgent prompting by Al Jackson's emphatic drumming.

Of the other non-originals, a sparse reading of Chuck Willis's 1956 hit It's Too Late is the least interesting track; his stripped down version of Solomon Burke's Home In Your Heart is notable for early bursts of the "gotta gotta gotta" improvisation, which would very soon after become a soul cliché and his version of black country singer O.B. McClinton's Keep Your Arms Around Me finds Booker T's insistent piano filling the background, and Packy Axton's tenor sax giving a running commentary on Otis's restrained celebration of his woman's love. But the highlights of the album are all to be found in Otis's originals, specifically Your One And Only Man and the incandescent Mr Pitiful. Chained And Bound, another original and a single in September 1964, sounds like Redding's hymn to Zelma, a man happy to be trussed up in monogamy. The strong horn lines and Cropper's confident guitar are the bricks and mortar of the piece. I Want To Thank You, also the B-side of Security, again finds Redding in happy mood, grateful to be hopelessly, helplessly in love and knowing that love is returned. Although not perhaps a well-known song, the instrumental balance is quintessential Stax – Booker T's piano fills the top of the track, Cropper's gutsy guitar and Duck Dunn's bass rock the bottom, the text-book horn phrases share centre-stage with Redding's voice and Al Jackson's drumming locks it all together.

The very title of Mr Pitiful describes the impact Redding had made on the soul market in the short space of time he'd been recording. It was a sobriquet laid on him by DJ A.C. "Moohah" Williams, who was tickled by the lovelorn scrapes into which – lyrically at least – Redding would plunge. The pitiful pleading, the testifying, the get-down-on-mah-knees-and-beg-to-you-darlin' heartbreak, these were traits of a man in constant emotional torment. Cropper thought the name a good song title, and together with Otis wrote the song in less than 15 minutes. The spirit of fun in which it was written is plain to hear. Superficially, the subject – a man laid low by repeated exposure to inconstant woman – is a sobering one, but the skittish pace, the manner in which the arrangement leads the band into a hop, two skips and a jump down to the end of each line and back up to the beginning of the next, Cropper's chimed guitar asides, Otis's "Can I explain to you?" uttered without rancour, all point to a joyful kind of piteousness. "Everything is going wrong, I've got to sing these sad songs to get back to her," Otis argues. Soul music's *raison d'être* has never been put more aptly or succinctly. Released as the flipside of That's How Strong My Love Is, Mr Pitiful eventually outperformed the A-side. That's How Strong reached Number 18 on the R&B charts and 74 on the pop charts; Pitiful peaked at 10 and 41 respectively.

Your One And Only Man, by contrast, is "Mr Pitiful" at his most desperate, as Redding tries to make the woman of his dreams and desires understand the depth of his passion. He does this by laying out the rules of engagement, demanding undivided love and loyalty. The rich horn section, Cropper's chording and frills, the tension built by Al Jackson's drum rolls, underpinned by Duck Dunn's huge performance on bass guitar – all make for a great soul group performance. They were right on song and there were many, many more to follow.

5 Otis Blue

OTIS REDDING SINGS SOUL BALLADS HAD SWEPT aside any remaining doubts at Stax about his potential appeal and had disseminated the word into the soul world. But this was, still, a comparatively small world. In the wider context of 1965, Beatlemania had gripped the USA, almost anything British would sell (Peter & Gordon, Herman's Hermits, The Dave Clark Five) and the biggest-selling "black" label was not Stax, or Atlantic, but Berry Gordy's stable of Detroit labels, notably Tamla and Motown. This lurch towards poppier sounds had left a void in R&B which was being best exploited by the Hardest Working Man In Showbusiness, James Brown. His music was going in the opposite direction – becoming "blacker", rhythmically more emphatic, and with lyrics in touch with the street. Born in South Carolina but raised, like Otis, in Georgia, Brown had preceded Redding out of the Macon circuit and on to the wider American platform. He remembered Redding from the talent shows at the Douglass Theatre and after These Arms Of Mine, Otis had travelled up to the Apollo Theatre in Harlem to appear on a James Brown-headlined show. In *Godfather Of Soul*, his ghosted autobiography, Brown describes how Otis arrived without any music charts for the house band, so he had saxophonist St. Clair Pinckney, his bandleader at the time, write out the charts – "The first ones he ever had, and I think they really helped him get over."

What really got Otis "over" was his third album and its hit singles. Over 35 years after its release, *Otis Blue* still regularly features in "Best Ever Album" polls – 23 in NME's 1985 poll, 31 in the 1995 MOJO magazine poll. Released in September 1965, the LP quickly came to be regarded as his masterpiece and the artistic and commercial pinnacle of Southern soul. The "Stax Sound" did not get much better than this. Not so self-consciously dominated by slow tempi as *Soul Ballads*, the balance it struck between uptempo tracks, mid-tempo stomps and ballads, and the way in which the songs were sequenced, is nigh-on perfect. The ghost of Sam Cooke throws a reverential, rather than a morbid, shadow over the album. Cooke had been shot dead in December 1964; Otis started the album in April 1965, recording the bulk of it in July of that year. The record comprised three Sam Cooke songs and another soul song first associated with Solomon Burke, a B.B. King blues, a fellow Stax writer-singer's best-known hit, three originals including one co-written with Jerry Butler, and, in a clever accident after a final, desperate search for material, a Motown cover and a version of a British group's contemporary hit. This broadening of material made Redding all the more accessible to the white, album-buying rock market, which although in its infancy was becoming a strong and important force in the marketplace.

The slower tunes on his early 45s, such as These Arms Of Mine and Pain In My Heart, had established Otis as a singer hiding – none too well – an aching vulnerability behind powerful and emotionally intense singing. These first soul-market hits and the second album, *Sings Soul*

Ballads, had concentrated almost wholly on similar songs. Yet the biggest hit thus far had also been the fastest cut, Mr Pitiful, the one which exuded the most fun and self-awareness. Contributing mightily, too, was the Stax house band, which had gelled into a strong, cohesive unit, whose ensemble playing was central not just to Otis Redding's success, but to that of Sam And Dave, Eddie Floyd and all of the many stars who walked through the doors of the old movie house on East McLemore.

Considering its place and stature in soul music's history, the surviving participants in the recording of *Otis Blue* make its creation sound much like a happy accident. Wayne Jackson's view of Redding's sessions was that "Otis came in the studio and started making songs, putting songs together out of the top of his head. They came together and whoever packaged them, I guess, put 'em together. Otis never thought, 'I'll do an album called *Otis Blue*.' He was just cutting complete songs."

The first complete song he cut for the third album, in April 1965, was one he'd written one drunken evening with Jerry Butler in a hotel room in Buffalo, New York. I've Been Loving You Too Long became the biggest hit single

Otis Redding had while he was alive, reaching Number 2 on the R&B chart and 21 on the pop chart. Butler, like Sam Cooke, was proving to be an influence on Redding in more than purely musical terms. Two years older than Otis, Butler had been born in Sunflower, Mississippi but had moved north to Chicago with his family at the age of three so his knowledge of Redding's South was scant. He'd sung in several church choirs and with the Northern Jubilee Gospel Singers before moving to the Traveling Spiritualist Church Choir, where he met Curtis Mayfield. Meanwhile, he had graduated from the Washburne Trade School and was apprenticed to the catering trade while playing dates with The Roosters, a group up from Chattanooga, Tennessee which, with Mayfield, became The Impressions.

Although Butler soon left The Impressions, he and Mayfield remained good friends and in 1961 formed Curtom Music Publishing. (Sam Cooke's SAR was already established.) Butler's grounding in the catering business gave him a grasp of fiscal matters and his subsequent development in the '70s of The Butler Songwriters' Workshop, based in Chicago, and of a beverages distribution company, indicated a business mind as sharp as Sam Cooke's.

Redding was also keen to give himself a firm business foundation and men like Cooke and Butler were solid role models. Butler, who thought songwriting was a communal rather than solitary occupation, was attracted by Otis's fund of song ideas. Though by far the best known, I've Been Loving You Too Long was not the only song they wrote together – (Nobody Ever Loved Anybody) The Way I Loved You, a powerful ballad which appeared on Butler's *Dream Merchant* album, was another. (Just as Redding's career was taking off big time in 1965, Butler's was hitting the skids. Vee-Jay, the label for which he'd reeled off a series of hits from 1960 onwards, went bust and he was left searching for a new style. He found it in 1968 courtesy of Kenny Gamble, Leon Huff, Thom Bell and the Philadelphia Sound.)

Otis recorded I've Been Loving You Too Long twice. The first version for the single is good, but the album version benefited from performance of the song on the road. Already an archetypal Southern soul ballad, the pace is slower as his restrained, mournful vocal rises and falls through a series of crescendos, which inexorably build in intensity. At every peak, Redding's voice reaches for the top note, falling off it with a quivering trill that speaks of real emotion. At the end, as the horn fanfare builds in volume, Isaac Hayes's piano and Al Jackson's booming bass drum add to the drama. (The song's potential for dynamic live performance is obvious: frequently covered, the most famous version is Ike And Tina Turner's for their *Outta Season* album in 1969, which on-stage in the '70s verged on the pornographic as Tina Turner, stroking the microphone in unambiguous fashion, writhed, groaned and squealed her way through the song, finally seeming to fellate the mic.)

So much for the singles. The album started where *Soul Ballads* had left off – in the guise of 'Mr Pitiful'. Ole Man Trouble, an Otis original with uncredited lyrics from his Macon buddy Sylvester Huckaby, is a blues launched by Steve Cropper's choking sob of a guitar break, announcing the horns' opening notes. Otis demands an even break from the devils that beset him and, as Booker T.'s organ chords fill the background, the track builds to the horn solo, mournful yet swelling with pride. "We didn't have the luxury of cutting tracks," Jackson observed. "We cut songs in total. Sometimes it would take several hours to put it all together because Otis was inventing stuff, we all were inventing stuff as we went along. We might need a horn line so we'd fool around for an hour sittin' around and scratchin' our heads until somebody came up with it. But it was a lot of fun, there wasn't any stumblin' around much. It moved pretty fast."

Isaac Hayes agreed. "Yeah, 'cos he knew what he wanted. And he had everybody's undivided attention. He'd give us the tune and we'd run it over and we'd perfect it as we taped it. When you got reliable people like Al Jackson on drums, who held everything together, it just fell in place. He worked a lot with Cropper. I always wondered, if he had lived, how many more contributions he would have made, how much more influence he would have had in this industry."

When Otis arrived in Memphis for a session, he usually had an album's worth of ideas that he and Cropper would work on for a couple of days before presenting them to the house band. "The tunes that [Otis] wrote, I think he lived them," Isaac Hayes said, talking about Respect, the second track on *Otis Blue*. There are several explanations of its creation. Hayes admitted he'd be "going out on a limb" but "it might have been the way he was expressing himself about his home life". It was certainly one of Redding's favourite songs – he liked the groove and the lyric and said it took him a day to write, about 20 minutes to arrange and was cut in one take. His friend and road manager, Earl "Speedo" Simms, told Peter Guralnick that it had been brought along by his group for their session at Stax. Simms's voice did not record well so Otis, who turned the ballad into an uptempo stomp, recorded it and took the writer's credit too. Drummer Al Jackson had yet another take on the song's genesis, recalling to Jann Wenner of Rolling Stone a conversation with Otis about the vicissitudes of life, during which he said, "What are you griping about, you're on the road all the time, all you can look for is a little respect when you come home." Redding, Jackson said, wrote the tune from that conversation. "We laughed about it quite a few times. In fact, Otis laughed about it all the way to the bank."

Steve Cropper reckoned between a half and three quarters of all their songs came from a phrase in a conversation. That way the titles had a genuine ring to them, and were readily identifiable to DJs and record-buyers alike. Whatever the inspiration for Respect, the finished track is a thundering success. Driven by Al Jackson's battering four-to-the-bar snaps on the snare drum – the trick which gives many of the great Motown hits of the '60s their insistent call to the dancefloor – and machine-gun rolls with Duck Dunn's pounding bass, Respect is a track with a lot of bottom. Atop the rhythmic stomp, the horns harmonise on a monumental riff which has become a blueprint for the arrangement of soul horns.

Redding's reading of the lyric veers from the reasonableness of a man who will deny his woman nothing her heart desires – "Hey little girl, you're as sweet as honey/And I'm about to give you all my money" – to the simmering anger of a partner who thinks he's so poorly regarded that he has to demand respect. You can almost hear the front door slam as he arrives back home from a hard day at the microphone. A Number 4 R&B hit and 35 pop hit in the US, Respect earned its writer precisely that.

Much has been made of the record's political meaning, at the time of civil rights and black power move-ments, and of how Aretha Franklin's substantially different version of the song in 1966 became an anthem of black pride. But what sparked The Queen Of Soul's interest in the song at first was the resonance the lyric had for her domestic situation. "Of course Aretha picked up on that too," Isaac Hayes twinkled. "I know she was singing to a man. I won't call his name. You know about that situation." (Her producer, Jerry Wexler, had banned her husband, Ted White, from the studio after he disrupted her first Muscle Shoals recording sessions.)

The rest of *Otis Blue* is cover versions. Of the three Sam Cooke songs on the album, A Change Is Gonna Come and Shake had been released as a Cooke single by RCA in December 1964, days before his death. Shake was a pulsing dance track which Otis makes into an even more aggressive piece, with his earthier, more guttural delivery. Al Jackson's drumming is outstanding – busy as a steam engine's pistons in the verse and a model of how to maintain momentum during the arrangement's many breaks. Cropper's choppy chording and Dunn's locomotive bass underline the motor functions of the rhythm section, while the horns punctuate each vocal line. But the track belongs to Al Jackson. In the spring of 1967, Shake was released as a single and sold respectably, reaching 16 R&B and 47 pop.

The second Cooke cover is a very different animal.

A Change Is Gonna Come signalled a switch of direction, or more properly a return to roots, for the former gospel prodigy. Both lyric and melody burst with hope yet the contemplation of better days that lay ahead is heavily coloured by a sense of weariness, and of sadness for those who've not been able to make the journey or who have been lost along the way. In Redding's version, a mournful, gospel-tinged horn opening with Wayne Jackson's trumpet piercing the heart leads into the steady verses. Cropper's guitar and Hayes's piano further set the mood, while in the bridge the horns return to dramatise the lyric up to the first climax, with Jackson's drums and the horns beating a tattoo. Where Cooke's reading is restraint and contemplation, a quiet explanation of a state of affairs, Redding's taps into the puzzle of the lyric, of how man could have been allowed to get into this situation in the first place. Surely life did not have to be this way? Instead of using Cooke, the lead singer of The Soul Stirrers, as his model, Redding harks back to the more extravagant extemporisers, like Archie Brownlee of The Five Blind Boys Of Mississippi. His vocal asides and exclamations are the very stuff of gospel. With a running time of over four minutes it was the longest recording Otis had made. But every second of the transformation is absorbing. Wonderful World, the third and final Cooke cover on *Otis Blue*, was one of the most overtly 'pop' songs either recorded. Redding's is by far the rootsiest version, replacing Cooke's smooth delivery with a jaunty and engagingly enthusiastic treatment. A chunky rhythm is offset by the horns' shadings and ends with the trumpet soloing behind Redding's ad-libs.

Otis's reading of Solomon Burke's Down In The Valley is reasonably faithful to the original, while he went back to the blues again for a grinding remake of B.B. King's Rock Me Baby. His interpretation of the lyrics make crystal clear the original vernacular meaning of "rock and roll" – hot, steamy sex. "Play the blues, Steve," he commands before Cropper's rare, fluent solo. In common with most of the tracks on this third album, the fade suggests that Otis and the band will be grooving on the song long after the tape has run out. The ability to remake apparently unsuitable songs and thereby give a new dimension to them is apparent on My Girl.

By and large, the team at Stax steered clear of Motown covers because they were too 'pop'. This did not stop them studying how lyrics were constructed and how words fitted snugly with the rhythm pattern. As sung by The Temptations, Smokey Robinson and Ronald White's My Girl is a delicate hymn of thanks to the good Lord for sending such a sweet-natured beauty. The slight rasp in David Ruffin's tenor, the quintet's deft harmonies, Melvin Franklin's rich bass – all produce a feeling of contentment in love. The instrumental track is full – Motown rarely made better use of the Detroit Symphony Orchestra's string section – yet never intrusive. Hard to better, which Stax did not attempt to do. Instead, while following the very basic arrangement, they made an entirely different song.

Trimmed to its essentials, Otis's My Girl opens with Duck Dunn's bass and Steve Cropper's guitar as though they are going to try to match Motown sweetness for sweetness. Then Al Jackson's snare clatters in and we're transported to a completely different territory as the grainier texture of the treatment becomes quickly apparent. The horn section replaces both The Temptations' harmonies and the Detroit strings, their strong blowing and Otis's eagerness with the lyrics turning the song into one in which a powerful, upright pride in My Girl is being expressed, as opposed to the joyful exuberance with which The Temptations finish. Their My Girl had been a Number 1 pop and R&B hit in January 1965. Otis's version, not released in the States as a single at the time for that reason, was his first major breakthrough in the UK, where The Temptations' original had not sold quite so exhaustively, and reached Number 11 in January 1966.

A version of You Don't Miss Your Water, the ballad that had brought William Bell to Stax, again showed how Otis's thick and solid tone, and the muscularity with which he attacked the lyrics, could reinvent a song. As Cropper gently lays out the chords and Dunn's bass keeps the slow flow, the horns add gospel amens. Here, Otis's final improvisations on the fade are given a sudden, unexpected boost by Al Jackson building a fast crescendo with unison snare and tom-tom beats and, just as it starts to fade, the track hits a new peak.

The final cover version was perhaps the most audacious. For years, British artists had been copying American songs, be they jazz musicians in the '40s and '50s, folk, skiffle or rock'n'roll singers in the '50s and early '60s or the beat groups of the '60s from The Beatles and The Rolling Stones down. In fact, so commonplace was the practice, and so different from the original was Otis Redding's version of The Rolling Stones' Satisfaction, that many Americans thought the Stones had covered Redding's song rather than vice versa. There were many precedents – the Stones' early two albums were awash with remakes of blues, R&B and soul ballads – and they had already used Redding originals Pain In My Heart and That's How Strong My Love Is.

The idea for the cover version came from Cropper and Booker T., Otis told Jim Delehant. During a break in the sessions, Cropper, searching for material to record, had the notion that Otis could make something of the Stones' Satisfaction. While the singer was out of the studio, Cropper played it to the band and they started to work on it. Otis hadn't heard the Stones song and when he did, he didn't like it. "I use a lot of words different from the Stones version – that's because I made them up." Which led to the rumours that he'd written the song first. As Al Jackson pointed out: "He wrote his version."

"We were always searching for a pop song that Otis could get into so we could break him on pop radio, because the only stations that would play him were WLAC, WDIA, stations like that," Steve Cropper explained. The guitarist sat down at a record player and transcribed what he thought were the words – "I don't think we got them exactly the way they were on the record but they were close enough." Before they'd cut the track Otis threw away the lyric sheet and paid only lip service, as it were, to the Stones' words. "We kept the basic guitar line and bass line but we kinda changed the tempo, added kind of a funky thing in the middle."

What the *Otis Blue* version of Satisfaction lacks in preparation and rehearsal it makes up for in sheer raw energy and no small amount of flying by the coat-tails – the first break in the arrangement clearly comes as a big surprise to Otis. The horn section – playing at one point what sounds like part of the theme to the Batman TV series – and Al Jackson's fevered drumming, especially during the final breakdown when his bass drum is battering eight beats to the bar behind the trumpets' trilled triplets, urge Otis to wilder, tougher interjections. Or as Isaac Hayes simply put it: "He took that Stones tune and took it over and made it a whole other thing." Released as a single in the

US in February 1966, it was significantly unlike the Stones' version to become a Number 31 pop hit there and reached 4 on the R&B charts. (The English group's original had been a pop Number 1 in June 1965.)

Redding released another single that year which had not been included on the album. Most of the up-tempo songs he had recorded were inimitable readings of other people's songs – his originals tended to be ballads. I Can't Turn You Loose was an early exception to this rule. The motor of the song comes from Cropper and Duck Dunn riffing in unison on guitar and bass guitar in front of Jackson's stomping four-on-the-floor drumming. The song's heart is expressed by the strong horn riff, proud and upright, while its soul springs from Redding's expostula-tory singing. He fights to get the words out quickly enough, as though there is simply too much emotion for him to express coherently. On-stage, I Can't Turn You Loose was taken at an even more frenzied pace. Perhaps it was appre-hension about this roaring full-out stomp that kept it relatively low on the pop chart at Number 85, rising to Number 11 R&B. Otis's road bass player, McElvoy Robinson, and Steve Cropper were listed as co-writers, as indeed they were on the flip, the ballad Just One More Day, which would provide the opening track to his fourth LP, *The Soul Album*.

Like many early Motown and, indeed, '60s soul albums generally, *Otis Blue* did not feature a photograph of the singer on either front or back of the sleeve, contemporary marketing logic being that the portrait of a black man might deter potential white American buyers. The album had been put together in two hectic days, the process helped by Atlantic's ace engineer/producer Tom Dowd, who had recently installed a new desk at the studio. This was by no means the normal speed of recording at Stax because many of the musicians had evening gigs with their groups. "We would probably do two songs in a day and then me and Duck would have to go and work at a club," Wayne Jackson said. "We had to leave at eight o'clock to be at work at nine. Then we'd usually have to be back at Stax at 11 am. Sometimes we would start then, sometimes we wouldn't start until one or two in the afternoon when everybody showed up if they'd stayed up all night and been drunk. And we had to all be there. So the ones that got there early might be drunk when the others got sober and showed up! So it was kind of a loose train. But we would all eventually get there and be same place, same time, same ideas, turn on the machine and you go to work."

"Otis's stuff was a little bit more intricate . . . sorta like, stump the horn players," Steve Cropper remembered. "He liked to come up with things to see if they could play it."

"There were no planning sessions," Jackson added. "He and Steve spent a lot of time talking about stuff. We just went in and did it. Stax was that way. When all the really great stuff at Stax was done, before they got a lot of money and offices and had people standing around with their hand out, briefcases and secretaries and stuff like that, and ruined the atmosphere of the place. When the good stuff was done there it was done quick. Everybody would show up to the studio around noon or one o'clock, and we'd get everything turned on and somebody would have a song, it might be David Porter or Isaac Hayes working with Sam And Dave, or some artist would be there, William Bell, he'd have this song, and it was a big group effort. Everybody just jumped in and stood around the piano while Isaac would play the song. Duck would learn the bass line and Al would find out what he was gonna do, and we'd fix the horn lines and be getting ready to do it and it would just build up. It would start with bones that somebody brought and the muscle and sinew and flesh and skin would be put on it while we were standing there and the monster would rise and live! Somehow."

6 The Soul Lexicographer

FOR STAX, THE BREAKTHROUGH REPRESENTED by Otis Redding's six R&B chart entries in 1965 and the impression *Otis Blue* had made at home and abroad was both a vindication and a warning. The sound and feel of the house band had long ago sent Atlantic's Jerry Wexler scurrying down to Memphis with a contract formalising the arrangement between the labels and with a new artist, Wilson Pickett, for Stax to work with. This meant that the Stax sound was heard on many Atlantic singles, and not just Otis Redding's albums, which were released on the Atco subsidiary. Pickett had two R&B hit singles that year and the second, Don't Fight It, reached as high as Otis's best effort, Respect; the former Falcon also had the Stax Studio's only Number 1 of the year with In The Midnight Hour, co-written by Steve Cropper and Eddie Floyd.

"I really didn't know who Wilson was," Cropper remembered. "We had access to [Estelle Axton's Stax] record shop, so I started finding things he had sung on." What he heard was a "wonderful" gospel-trained voice, "great chops", that reached really high but was also thick and gruff; his scream was the equal of James Brown's. But what Cropper focused on were the repetitive chants on the fades of his tracks, often repeated a dozen times or more. The phrase "midnight hour" frequently featured – "It seemed to be his trademark and just sparked me."

And at the end of the year, Isaac Hayes and David Porter were put to work with the duo Sam Moore and Dave Prater, a partnership which would for the next two years dominate gritty Southern soul with a series of blistering Stax-produced records. These, too, would be assigned to Atlantic.

As well as new acts on the roster, the backroom staff was swollen by an influx of out of town talent, notably Alvertis Isbell, a DJ from Washington DC who joined as head of promotion. Al Bell, as he was customarily known, quickly became a writer and producer, a talent scout, a wheeler and dealer and vice president, the first black man among the label's loosely structured management hierarchy. One of his first moves had been to bring Eddie Floyd, a singer-writer he'd known in Washington, to the label. Floyd's Knock On Wood, co-written one stormy night with Cropper and Wayne Jackson in Memphis's soon to become internationally notorious Lorraine Motel, was another Stax and Southern soul staple.

The deal between Stax and Atlantic was essential, not least because Tamla Motown had hit another incredibly rich seam of R&B and pop hits. "[Motown] was totally different," Sam Moore of Sam And Dave said. "Because Hayes and Porter was with Sam And Dave, we came over with a sound that since then everyone has impersonated, imitated, ripped-off, any of the above. At that time, we didn't think like that. We were focused on travelling and playing. We didn't know what records were actually happenin.' We heard more about what Ike And Tina Turner had done than what Motown was doin.'"

At the time, Motown was taking up an awful lot of

chart space. In 1965, records by The Temptations, Junior Walker & The All Stars, Marvin Gaye, The Supremes and The Four Tops occupied the Number 1 place on the R&B charts for 27 weeks, over half the year. And the label's success was not limited to the ethnic chart. The Supremes had three Number 1 pop hits in the US that year – Stop! In The Name Of Love, Back In My Arms Again, I Hear A Symphony – The Four Tops and The Temptations one each. The inimitable and iconoclastic James Brown, steadily reinventing himself from soul balladeer through Mr Dynamite and The Hardest Working Man In Show Business to become The Godfather Of Soul, was at Number 1 for a total of 14 weeks with just two King singles – Papa's Got A Brand New Bag and I Got You (I Feel Good). Records by Little Milton and Fontella Bass on the Checker label out of Chicago occupied the top spot for seven weeks. Stax, it seemed, still had plenty of room for improvement.

And it was playing on the minds of the creators of the Stax sound. As Otis told Jim Delehant: "Motown does a lot of overdubbing. It's mechanically done. At Stax the rule is: Whatever you feel, play it."

At 926 East McLemore, everything was recorded at

the same time, there would be three or four takes and a playback and the best one would be chosen. Otis explained that if somebody did not like a line in the song, they'd go back and cut the whole thing again. "Yesterday, we cut six songs in five hours and they'll all be in the album," was Redding's description of the day's work.

When Jerry Wexler was down in Memphis for a Wilson Pickett session, Steve Cropper asked him what made the Motown records so commercial. One thing to look at, Wexler said, was the metre of the lyrics. The words always fell with great emphasis on the up and down beat, they never slipped between the beats. So when Cropper and Eddie Floyd worked on In The Midnight Hour the lyrics were written to land like lead weights on the four beats of each bar. When the time came to record the song, Wexler, to get the feel that he thought would be right for the song, for Pickett and for the demands of the commercial marketplace, gave an impromptu demonstration of the latest dance craze in the Northern clubs, The Jerk. And it gave the Booker T. And The MG's rhythm section the delayed-beat groove that makes the rhythm appear to lean heavily on the downbeat.

When pressed today, Stax artists, producers and writers will insist that they felt no rivalry towards Berry Gordy's labels from Detroit, because Motown's music was aimed at a white pop market and therefore not seen as direct competition. At the time, however, there was clearly an awareness of what was happening up in Detroit.

1965 had also seen the young partnership of Isaac Hayes and David Porter reach full spate. "We wrote the tunes from direct inspiration," Hayes said. "Just like when I came with the title B.A.B.Y. for Carla [Thomas]. She was my girlfriend then. She used to call me 'Baby' all the time. And she would sleep down at the studio, sleep on the organ stool, whatever, just hang with me like that. I remember Al Jackson said, 'Well, you got her trained now, dontcha?' I said, 'Well . . .'. He said, 'But you just wait, it's gonna change!' But at the time it was bliss and that's how that tune B.A.B.Y. came about. When Something Is Wrong With My Baby came from David Porter's wife. We were standing one day, couldn't think of anything, so he went home. He was tired, I was tired, and he said when he got home his wife said [Isaac assumes a gentle, feminine, caressing voice],

'What's wrong, is something wrong with my baby?' Started massaging his shoulders and he said, 'That's it!' And he called me up on the phone, 'Ike! Ike! I'll be over in five minutes, man, I gotta tell ya I got some lyrics, man, it's awesome, it's awesome!' And he came over and in my living room we started working on it and we wrote the whole thing there. That's the one thing about soul music. You write it based on your personal experiences and inspirations and I'm sure that was the deal with Otis."

The genesis of Sam And Dave's Hold On! I'm Comin' – Porter's reply, from the toilet, to urgent requests that he get back into the studio and cut the Number 1 R&B hit – is well known. That aside, Hayes and Porter had quite formal work practices in the studio. "Isaac did the arranging and putting the voices to the horn lines," Sam Moore explained. "We used three horns – two saxes and a trumpet. In the earliest part of our career we would cut live, record live with everybody being there. That started taking a little of the strength out of us. We were maybe trying to get four, five or six songs out at every recording session. After a while, after you pass three, you in trouble because your throat becomes very tired and, especially if you coming off the road, you can't sometimes pass three. 'OK, we'll come back tomorrow and finish up.'

"Now when you go back tomorrow, you've got to try to match what you sounded like because, if you don't, it's gonna sound real off. So, as things got better, studio got bigger, got more tracks, we went to eight, 16 then 24. I don't think Dave and I were there for 24. And David [Porter] used to get inside, behind the partition with us, he would stand right in front of me. David's thing was never leave anything unsaid. Fill in, do a lotta fill-ins.

"If there was, say for instance [sings the following very straight], 'Don't you ever, feel sad, Lean on me, when times get bad, When the day comes and you're down, And you in trouble you better, Hold on, I'm comin.' Don't do it that dry, put something in it, complete the line. And this [his index finger and thumb on each hand tease out the line] meant stretch the line. This [index finger and thumb on one hand slowly clamp like a vice] meant shorten the word, don't just linger with one word. For instance, we first sang, 'When something is wrooooong [holds note] with my baby.' Wrong. He didn't want that. He wanted, 'When something is wrong [pause] with my baby.'

"Same thing happened with Soul Man. When the instrumental part came along, I was standing there and I wasn't saying anything. Porter was [mouths 'Sing something! Sing something!', gets excited] and I shouted, 'Play it, Steve!', because he scared me. Panic! We went into the engineering room and believe it or not, all afternoon and almost for the next day they sat and they played that over, trying to decide whether to take that out. They were concerned about singling out one person. I explained, 'Well, David was screaming in my face so I panicked. And the first person I saw was Steve and I just screamed it out loud.' Then next time I heard the finished product, they'd left it in and it actually made Steve Cropper a household name, didn't it? Someone said to me a short while ago, 'If you had only kept your damn mouth shut!'" (In fact, Redding had already immortalised Cropper with a similar cry at the start of the guitar solo to Rock Me Baby.)

Sam And Dave also reaped the benefits of Otis's development of the Stax horn style. "He sang gospel so I think those horns could have substituted the vocal backing," Hayes said. "He never had vocal backing, so the horns substituted. As a result it brought the horns to the forefront. And those lines [he hums Mr Pitiful] were rhythmic. When he sang 'Fa fa-fa fa-fa fa fa fa fa' the horns went 'da da-da da-da da da da da', that slurring little thing. It was an image, pure image. But I watched Otis and listened to him, how he did these things – 'daa, dun, daaan!' – Mr Pitiful, I played on all of those things. I learned. I learned to take liberties. I learned just watching what he did. Because I was a bit of an introvert when I first went in there, because I was on unfamiliar ground. And so when I started feeling my oats, I learned to stretch and reach by watching Otis and listening to what he did.

"When it came to music, he was totally uninhibited. He knew he couldn't sometimes pronounce a word grammatically correct or enunciate it properly but he got the idea and the feel across and that's the most important thing when you're talking about arts. To get emotion. To extract emotion from people. To expel your emotions and that's what he did and he did it by way of his performance, by way of the rhythm that drove it and by way of the horn line. And I learned that from him. It's like an extension of one's personality, when you create a mood."

If 1965 had been a year of breakthrough for Stax, 1966

was the year of expansion and consolidation. For the cover of Otis's fourth LP, *The Soul Album*, the blonde-haired, white-skinned model bathed in indigo light of *Otis Blue* was replaced by a black-haired, brown-eyed, brown-skinned model in loose head scarf. But the album it announced was not appreciably "blacker" than its predecessor. If anything, it's bluesier. The 11 tracks were again a balance of five Stax originals and six cover versions. Just One More Day, which had already been available as the flip of I Can't Turn You Loose, was a typical Redding ballad with Cropper's guitar making some particularly inventive tones (he'd clearly been listening to white rock and pop guitarists) and the organ pipier than usual – more like a Farfisa than a Hammond. Al Jackson's contribution is unusually restricted to hi-hat and lightly used brushes, until the final extemporisation as he urges on the singer and horns. The success of My Girl prompted the use of another Smokey Robinson song written for The Temptations. The treatment of It's Growing is even less like the Motown blueprint than My Girl had been. All subtlety and pastel shadings are cast aside for the broad sweep of horn colours and Jackson's hard-socked snare drum.

The highlights of the album are his contemplative, surprisingly gentle reading of the ballad Cigarettes And Coffee, Good To Me and a more typical, increasingly desperate version of Nobody Knows You (When You're Down And Out). There is not much in the canon of this big-voiced big man that can truly be said to be understated but Cigarettes And Coffee comes as close as anything can do. The smoky, late-night atmosphere is created by the horn section and a busy piano, while Duck Dunn's slow, steady bass line and Jackson's boomingly solid drums exude a relaxed weariness. After Nobody Knows You, Good To Me returns immediately to the measured and more carefully modulated soul ballad style. Taken at a funereal pace, this gentle celebration of constancy – they've been together for "20 long years" and he's about to go for 40 more – was written with Julius Green of The Mad Lads.

Scratch My Back is altogether more skittish, with the horn section's cock-a-doodling playing the rooster loose in the barnyard and Cropper's undulating, reverberating guitar sashaying by their side. A rather perfunctory remake of Roy Head's Treat Her Right, which sounds leaden, a shade too four-square on the beat, leads into three final Stax-based songs. Eddie Floyd and Al Bell's Everybody Makes A Mistake is a soul ballad of regret at his loss of a woman while he was out playing fast and loose on the streets. It is, again, a moving, emotionally exposed performance with a wonderful fade as the trumpet mournfully echoes Redding's plight. Quite the opposite is Any Ole Way, a Redding/Cropper collaboration used as the flip of the Satisfaction single. It has an untypically jaunty pace and a very "pop" melody and arrangement. Finally, a reading of Wilson Pickett's 634–5789, Eddie Floyd/Steve Cropper's phone number Stax standard, is "straighter", the rhythm more evenly weighted through each bar's four beats. There was, of course, a Sam Cooke cover – Chain Gang, which adds little to the original, though one can visualise Redding tearing up a storm on-stage with it.

Redding's live set had by 1966 become a genuine revue. Although it was not released until after his death, the recordings of his show at the Whiskey A GoGo on Los Angeles's Sunset Strip on April 8–10, 1966 is typical of contemporary performances. "Oh, high energy, just like he was behind the mic," Isaac Hayes said. "High energy and that band was the same, they had those routines. Those were the days of the big bands – when I say big bands I mean a front line with the brass and reeds, the baritone sax. Joe Tex, Sam And Dave, James Brown had their bands and Otis had his. Those were the heavy hitters and, boy, they were so dynamic. They had their routines and Otis, right in the middle, doin' his thing. It was something to see, it was somethin' to see and people would be on their feet."

The great soul revues of the '60s had their roots in the '50s rock'n'roll bands of Fats Domino (coached by the outstanding musical director Dave Bartholomew), of Little Richard's Upsetters, of Ray Charles's band going way back to Louis Jordan's Tympani Five in the late '40s. The well-rehearsed precision and skill of the James Brown Band had been a central feature in building his appeal from the mid-'50s onwards and, as Hayes observed, by the mid-'60s the bands of Joe Tex and Sam And Dave were every bit as electrifying. Some soul stars still were not keen on paying out for a regular band and would be happy to use pick-up musicians. But few singers had Solomon Burke's facility with a "borrowed band".

As Otis was not a great athlete, he did not have the suppleness of former boxers like Jackie Wilson or James

Brown. Hayes agrees: "James had all these slick moves and routines and the one-leg thing and stuff. Now, Otis sometimes got on one leg, he did it just to prove that he could do it. Oh yeah, he did that. [Laughs.] But his thang . . . Wilson Pickett had a routine like this [Isaac boogaloos, first to the right with his right knee bent and the heel thumping on each beat for a bar or two and then switching to the left leg; the arms, bent at the elbow with the fist just under the chin, follow suit.] Otis did it but stayed on one side. Temptations, they did it, too. They had that step. But when he came out, he commanded the audience's attention and I would not want to be on the show with him. I would not want to go after him. 'Cos there was nothing left – he would destroy an audience, destroy them."

To try to capture the power of his performances, Atlantic employed live recording specialist Wally Heider and Nesuhi Ertegun, who had cut the label's live jazz sides in the '50s, and Stax sent the MG's drummer, Al Jackson Jr. Otis had a nine-piece band, with a six-man horn section – Sammy Coleman and John Farris (trumpets), Robert Holloway, Robert Pittman and Donald Henry (tenor saxes) and Clarence Johnson Jr (trombone) – and basic rhythm section of Ralph Stewart (bass), James Young (guitar) and Elbert Woodson (drums). Young and Woodson proved particularly good in their own right and as faithful as possible to the studio work of Steve Cropper and Al Jackson Jr. On the day of the first night the band rehearsed from 2am until 10am, slept, started rehearsing again from 4pm until the crowd came into the club. Among the music business and film stars in the audience was Bob Dylan, who reportedly offered Redding some songs he'd just written ("Too many words, man," one can hear Otis say). In all, seven sets were recorded and judicious editing removed a noticeably out-of-tune trumpet.

The potential of live recording as a communicator of the thrill and appeal of a top soul singer had been made obvious in 1962 by James Brown's *Live At The Apollo*. The electricity of Redding live is as palpable on *At The Whiskey A GoGo*. He attacks everything with the highest enthusiasm imaginable and the excitement of the extended version, say, of Satisfaction, reduces him to barely comprehensible tumult. Redding's passion seems barely held in check by a band which is as eager as the singer to cut loose. The frantic pace of uptempo songs, such as I Can't Turn You Loose,

Mr Pitiful and (I Can't Get No) Satisfaction, which was in the charts at the time, places extra demands on the guitars and expanded horn section. I Can't Turn You Loose, which opens the live album, bursts into pulsating action, gripping the audience from the start with a furious energy and, through a series of false endings, holds on tight. His remodelling of Satisfaction is even more pronounced than on record. It becomes very obvious why, in the US, many folks thought the song was his.

The delayed beat used on many post-Midnight Hour Stax recordings has been added to the live arrangement of Pain In My Heart, increasing its drama. Otis sings the ballad as though it's three days old, not three years. His faithful rendering of another ballad, Just One More Day, suggests a preference for the slower songs. Any Ole Way retains its breezy mood but the vigour of live performance rids it of much of the fluffy feel of the studio arrangement. The song makes more sense as a stage song and coming after the three demanding songs – Mr Pitiful, Satisfaction and I'm Depending On You – simply gives his vocal cords a rest.

A voice from the audience yells for These Arms Of

A mid-'60s promotion shot
of Otis Redding

Otis Redding on the set of the TV show Ready Steady Go!, 1967

The stellar Stax writing partnership of Isaac Hayes (left) and David Porter

Cutting tracks in the converted Capitol movie theatre on East McLemore Avenue

Stax house band Booker T. And The MGs in action

Otis Redding with Atlantic producer and Stax fan Jerry Wexler

Otis Redding (left) in the Stax offices with label founder Jim Stewart, Rufus Thomas and Booker T. Jones. Seated is Carla Thomas

Sam Moore (seated) and Dave Prater: the soul men's live show made Otis work even harder

Otis Redding with MG's keyboard player Booker T. Jones during the Stax-Volt 1967 European tour. Carla Thomas is in the foreground

Otis Redding, the definitive Southern soul voice

Otis Redding on-stage with Booker T. And The MGs at Hunter College,
New York City, January 21, 1967, when Redding made a surprise appearance at
the Stax house band's gig

Mine, which is duly sung against a constant babble of voices in the background from a crowd that had come to party. So Otis keeps up with James Brown's innovations in funk with a version of Papa's Got A Brand New Bag. (An edited version was released as a single after Redding's death, reaching 10 on the R&B charts, 21 pop.) Respect, with a strange, jolting transition between the pomp of the horn riff and the guitar riff of the verses, sounds rather like a song coming apart at the seams, as though Otis and the band had tired of playing it on the road and were performing it out of duty until they could work out a fresh treatment.

A second volume from the live tracks was released by Atlantic in 1982 as *Otis Redding Recorded Live* and a slightly expanded version as *Good To Me: Live At The Whiskey A GoGo Volume 2* on Stax/Fantasy in 1992. The second selection from his three days' recording at the Whiskey gives plenty of illustrations of the spontaneity of Redding's performances – as opposed to the precision and reliability of James Brown's shows – and more ruthlessly exposes the shortcomings of the errant trumpeter. After Al "Brisco" Clark's introduction, based on Brown's "Are you ready for Star Time ..." format, there is another breezy I'm Depending On

You and then Your One And Only Man, which, lacking the control of the studio environment, is a bit of a mess. Otis's ineffable good humour and enthusiasm is plain to hear on his introduction to Good To Me, which was then a brand new song recorded at Stax only a few days earlier and worked up with the band during rehearsals. He follows it with another new song, Chained And Bound. Horns apart, this is a great soul ballad performance with guitarist James Young doing a very commendable impersonation of Cropper's style. Alternative versions of Pain In My Heart, These Arms Of Mine and I've Been Loving You Too Long, built into two massively dramatic crescendos, emphasise Redding's abiding ease and excellence with the soul ballad form.

Not every uptempo song was cranked up to a higher pace when Otis took it to the stage. I Can't Turn You Loose is less frenetic on the alternate live take than the version on the first album but the demonic groove on the long fade is awesomely hypnotic. After a straightforward romp through Security comes a real curiosity, a version of The Beatles' A Hard Day's Night. He performed the Lennon/McCartney song only once and never recorded it at Stax. The assumption that the lyric – "There's bin some hard day's night and I bin workin' just like a dog" – struck a chord with the drained singer and band. Subsequently, in the sessions for the next studio album recorded in August and September of 1966, he returned to The Beatles' songbook for Day Tripper.

Redding was a live performer of great energy and physicality – not in the sense of throwing himself about the stage, though there was a good amount of stomping about the place, but in putting that strong body into the song, of singing with his entire frame. He refashioned songs each time he sang them, lengthening one here, editing another with an impromptu cut there, depending on how the mood took him or how the set was going. "The most exciting thing that rock-worn room has ever harboured," noted Pete Johnson of the Los Angeles Times.

But Redding had some rivals close to home. A story goes that Otis, after closing the show behind Sam And Dave following a long, trying, tiring week at the Apollo, had ordered his manager, Phil Walden, never to book him on the same bill as Sam And Dave again. "That's an old joke," Sam laughs. "That's not really true. No. He liked that pressure in the early part of our careers." Their first tour together lasted 37 days, the first seven at the Apollo, after which Redding's voice was beat up bad. "These mother-fuckers are killing me," he said to Walden, and had Sam And Dave moved to close the first half of the show. Then he had them moved back to immediately before him where they would make him "work harder than I ever did in my life". At the end of the tour, Redding indeed told Walden he never wanted to go on the road with Sam And Dave again. Unfortunately, Phil had just signed the contracts for the Stax/Volt tour, which meant 30 days in Europe.

"Sam [Moore] wishes there was a rivalry between he and Otis but there was a huge gulf between he and Otis," Wayne Jackson said. "He knows that."

A month after the live recording, Otis was back at Stax recording My Lover's Prayer, the new ballad he'd written, which became a summer hit in 1966. It was quite at odds with their other sounds – Sam And Dave's Hold On! I'm Comin', Wilson Pickett's Ninety Nine And A Half Won't Do – but wholly in tune with the year's biggest Southern soul hit, and the first one to go Number 1 on the US pop charts, Percy Sledge's When A Man Loves A Woman.

My Lover's Prayer was a Number 10 R&B hit and 61 pop hit for Otis in June. A couple of months later, he went back to Memphis to record another ballad, which had the self-referential humour of Mr Pitiful. Fa-Fa-Fa-Fa-Fa (Sad Song), written by Redding and Cropper, makes fun of the singer's penchant for soul ballads. "I keep singing them sad, sad songs," he sings, "sad songs is all I know", the "fa-fa" vocal refrain is mimicked by the horn section. In the vamp, they moan in a mock-tearful bray.

"When he was in the studio," Jackson said, "he'd be stompin' around like he did, and when he'd hear a horn part he'd come stompin' over and sing it "fa-fa-fa-fa" right in your face. And we'd be . . ." (Jackson assumes the bug-eyed and tight-lipped look of a stunned cartoon character.) Suitably motivated, the horns would replicate Redding's voiced horn lines pretty much note for note. "The horn section, Andrew, Floyd and I, well, I had a very rounded tone for a trumpet and that blended well with the horns."

Indeed, the softer, warmer tone of Jackson's trumpet playing gave the section's sound a very close-knit overall pitch. "We used to have," Wayne Jackson recalled, "a guy from the local [musicians'] union hired as third trumpet sit in the corner at every session. We didn't let him play anything, he just had to be there to satisfy the union."

Although a smaller R&B hit than My Lover's Prayer, Sad Song was a bigger pop hit, reaching 29, and was the second single released off *The Otis Redding Dictionary Of Soul: Complete & Unbelievable*, the final solo album issued during his lifetime. The sessions for the album were long, some lasting 24 hours straight and another 24 to go to get the record done. Stimulants kept them going – like black beauty pills that would keep your eyes open for seven days and, even when you went home and lay down in bed, your eyes would still be locked open. "I remember one time I was having trouble keeping going and Wayne gave me something," saxophonist Andrew Love laughed, "and it was something! After the session I went straight home, got out the ladders and brushes and I painted my home from top to bottom! That was some time in, what, 1965–67. We was working just seven days a week non-stop."

Redding's use of open-tuned guitar when he was writing and his feeling for certain keys – A, E, F sharp – made his horn lines particularly testing, but he was a patient band-leader not given to explosions of rage. (The live recordings from the Whiskey A GoGo show how much latitude he allowed players.)

The second outstanding piece on *Dictionary* is his rearrangement of Try A Little Tenderness. A Tin Pan Alley standard written by Reg Connelly, James Campbell and Harry Woods, it was recorded in 1933 by Ted Lewis And His Band, then Ruth Etting, then by crooner Bing Crosby later in the '30s and Frank Sinatra in the '40s. It was a well-tested standard. Tenderness was, thinks Isaac Hayes, Otis's attempt to do with a standard what Sam Cooke had done with standards.

"We worked up Try A Little Tenderness," Hayes said, "that was [drummer] Al Jackson's genius, chick-ticka-chick-ticka, keep that rhythm going throughout. It was a jazz ballad. See, Otis was a Sam Cooke fan. And Sam Cooke did this thing, *Live At The Copa* . . . I think Sam did Try A Little Tenderness too." In fact, Cooke's *Live At The Copa* includes a medley of You Send Me and For Sentimental Reasons, with a couple of verses of Tenderness interpolated. "So Otis, he did it his way. He did it his style. It was just amazing."

"Al Jackson actually made a mistake," recalled Wayne Jackson. "He went to the double-time too soon and we were recording and it felt good so he kept it. Everything Otis Redding did was spontaneous. It was never planned or talked out."

Tenderness is a brilliant arrangement. The horn section's sentimental lament, based by Hayes on a mixture of the introduction to Cooke's A Change Is Gonna Come and a sentimental Stephen Foster-style melody, eases the door open. Cropper's sparingly strummed guitar and Duck Dunn's bass pushes it wider for Hayes and Booker T. at the piano and organ to join in; at the end of the first verse, Cropper and Love slip in jazzy inflections. At the start of the second verse, Al Jackson's rim taps on the four beats of the bar set a pace at odds with the reflective playing of the rest of the band. The intensity of the melody and playing gradually increases until Al Jackson lifts his left hand off the snare drum and hits full blown rimshots, socking the band to the fade. The speed of the transition from ballad to full-spate soul stomp is stunning. Again, you can only imagine them long after the fade still pounding on the groove, with the horns' volume building mightily, Hayes and Porter hitting their keys and stomping their feet, Dunn and Cropper hunching in concentration over guitar and bass, Jackson driving with increasing muscular urgency and, good God almighty, Otis himself, sweat pouring off him, as it invariably did, falling to his knees as he is engulfed by waves of passion and incoherent excitement.

Tenderness became a Number 4 R&B hit and 20 pop hit after its release in November 1966. Its flipside, I'm Sick Y'All, was Redding having yet another joke at his own expense after a brief illness. Written by Redding and Cropper with David Porter, its psychosomatic diagnosis attributes physical illness to emotional causes, while the grinding guitar/bass lines and opening horn statement, taken up later by organ, have the feel of incidental music to a scene in a B-movie thriller.

Other Redding originals on the 12-song *Dictionary* included Sweet Lorene, written with Hayes and Al Bell and using a tempo, arrangement and organ accents on the upbeat which give the track an identical feel to In The Midnight Hour. Hayes and David Porter were his co-writers on Love Have Mercy, the album's final track.

"He'd hang out with us. We'd go down the Four Way Grill, a soul food place, have a bite to eat," Hayes remembers. "I lived in one room at a boarding house. And they came to pick me up. Well, they . . . I thought David was coming to pick me up, we were hustling, struggling song-writers, but when I come down to the car Otis was sitting in the car with a gittar sittin' in his lap. And we started for the studio. I said, Man, I got this tune, and we pulled over to the side of the street and we started to work out this tune right there at the side of the street. I think it was Love Have Mercy. We wrote the song right there in the car."

Redding alone wrote the remaining originals. Remarkably varied in style, She Put The Hurt On Me synthesises old songs and current ideas into a new work. Redding added the briefly hip 1966 phrase "my baby socked it to me". He used it again in Hawg For You. Repetitions of the same or very similar phrases, of falling back on tried, tested terms when ad-libbing, laid Redding open to charges of an increasingly mannered style. This, the charges read, was done either deliberately, in which case he was pander-ing to a less sophisticated audience and generally rabble rousing, or it was accidental, in which case he had run out of ideas. There does seem to be a hurried and slightly unfinished feel to several of the tracks and it is likely that he was keen to get the project finished and get well. What is certainly true is that Redding's popularity meant that his signature improvisations – the "my-my-my-mys" and "gotta gottas" – were being expropriated by "soul" singers of whatever hue, turning them into clichés.

Finally, there was Ton Of Joy, a highlight on the album along with My Lover's Prayer and Tenderness. Pitched unusually near the top of Redding's range and, as a consequence, giving his voice a plaintive quality, it's an easy-paced four/four ballad sprung on Duck Dunn's bass guitar, with organ swells climaxing on each upbeat at the same moment as Cropper's muted electric guitar chords. The horns crisply comment in a track that is the better for its simplicity of arrangement.

Of the other reworkings, the country standard Tennessee Waltz (Sam Cooke had covered it in 1964) uses the ascending horn scales of I've Been Loving You Too Long in a slow ballad treatment; and then there's Lennon and McCartney's Day Tripper. Having dabbled with and discarded The Beatles' A Hard Day's Night, Redding attacks the song with the bullish determination last heard on Satisfaction. But again his voice seems in less than top condition and he sounds breathless, like a man not yet fully recovered from a flu-like illness. His aching version of Chuck Willis's You're Still My Baby, with Dunn's bass and Cropper's blues guitar, harks back to the slower pace of Rock Me Baby, the B.B. King remodel.

Released in October 1966, *The Otis Redding Dictionary Of Soul: Complete & Unbelievable* did indeed attempt to define "soul" in a glossary of terms, printed on the back of the sleeve. What it actually defined and attempted to phoneticise in jocular fashion were the vocables that Redding threw into his interpretations. Thus "Leetle" meant "just enough to make one want more", "Oh-mi" "to get it very quickly" and "gotta gotta" "not able to do without".

In the five and a half years of operation to the end of 1966, the Satellite, Stax and Volt labels had not enjoyed a strong track record with women singers. Mable John, sister to Little Willie John, and Ruby Johnson each had one significant hit in the first half of 1966 – Your Good Thing (Is About To End) and I'll Run Your Hurt Away respectively, both written by Isaac Hayes and David Porter – and a group called Barbara & The Browns, a quartet who really were all from the gospel singing Brown family, had a one-off pop Top 100 hit with Big Party in the spring of 1964. But releases on Dorothy Williams, Barbara Stephens, The Tonettes, Cheryl & Pam Johnson, Wendy Rene, who as Mary Frierson sang lead with The Drapels, and Deanie Parker met with no success.

In this period, only Carla Thomas made waves. Since Gee Whizz, the label's first hit with its third record released in November 1960, she had consistently made the charts with A Love Of My Own (March 1961), I'll Bring It Home To You (answering Sam Cooke's Bring It On Home To Me in October 1962), What A Fool I've Been (April 1963), I've Got No Time To Lose (July 1964), A Woman's Love (November 1964), How Do You Quit (Someone You Love) (February 1965), Stop! Look What You're Doin' (May 1965), Let Me Be Good To You (March, 1966) and B.A.B.Y. (July 1966). In that time only a handful of her singles had missed the charts and two of those were Christmas records. Since August 1960, when the second single out on Satellite, Cause I Love You, had featured Rufus and Carla, father and daughter had recorded several other singles which varied between the homespun and lovey-dovey and a more raucous, humorous style. In January 1967, her performance of another Isaac Hayes and David Porter song, Something Good (Is Going To

Happen To You), was edging her back into the charts and despite the pressure of work at Howard University in Washington DC, where she was studying for her Master's degree in English – most of her recording was done in the holidays – a new project gave hope for a new, mature phase in her career. During the Christmas vacation, she'd added her vocals to a series of duets with Otis Redding, his final act of 1966.

1967 was a big year for soul duets. At Tamla Motown, Marvin Gaye, who had already cut tunes with Mary Wells in 1964 and Kim Weston in 1964 and 1966, recorded a series of Valerie Simpson and Nikolas Ashford productions with Tammi Terrell, which defined the uptown soul duet. Although he regarded duets as fluffy novelties, Gaye's voice, a light tenor which slipped easily between a pleading urgency and that sweet-talkin' guy, was perfect for them. It was, perhaps, harder to hear the breast-beating misery or aggressive assertions of Otis Redding sharing the microphone with anyone, let alone with the gentler inflections of Carla Thomas. Much as she liked Otis, Carla could see the difficulties inherent in the project. Otis was not keen either. But label president Jim Stewart was. In fact, it was his idea. And the president's ideas usually get done.

The 11 basic tracks took three days to record. The majority of the songs had been written for and recorded by other acts, mostly Stax ones, but there was little need to work the raw material, other than to do some slight re-arranging. To get the juices flowing, Redding suggested a recent hit by Lowell Fulson. An extraordinarily adaptable blues-rooted guitarist, Fulson had played country blues and country, scored hits in the late '40s on the Downbeat and Swing Time labels with Three O'Clock Blues and Come Back Baby, and had three big R&B smashes in 1950 (Everyday I Have The Blues, Blue Shadow, Lonesome Christmas). He recruited Ray Charles into his band, giving the young pianist-singer-writer-arranger his first exposure to the rigours of life on the road. He then signed to Chess for another Top 5 R&B hit on their Checker subsidiary in 1954 with Reconsider Baby, which Elvis Presley covered. (Three O'Clock Blues and Everyday I Have The Blues became just as famous after B.B. King covered them.) But Fulson cut no more hits for Checker – the lights seemed to go out with the coming of rock'n'roll – and he did not find the switch again until his move from the Chess brothers' labels to Kent, part of the Bihari brothers' set-up. The dark soul-blues

Black Nights and Tramp, co-written with Jimmy McCracklin, were his final commercial flourish in 1965 and 1966.

Otis and Carla took a more skittish, jocular view of Tramp than had Fulson. In their hands it became a wonderfully light-hearted argument full of the badinage, insults and name-calling you might hear between inebriated couples in a bar. Sparked by Al Jackson's solid, brickhouse drumming, Carla lists long-held grievances against the no-good Georgia country boy who's got no dress sense, needs a haircut, is lazy and ain't got no money. "You're straight from the Georgia woods," she sneers. "That's good!" he returns, part in acknowledgement of his roots and part that she's getting into the role of an argumentative woman not happy with her no-good, backslidin' man. Otis's bragging reply, that he's a love man, cuts no ice. When she chides him that he probably doesn't have 25 cents to his name he reels off a list of the cars he owns: "six Cadillacs, three Lincolns, four Fords, six Mustangs, three Thunderbirds, a Mustang . . ." But most of all, he's a love man. Cropper's chopped guitar chords emphasise Jackson's drumming and the horn section splashes colour with a wonderfully upright riff, a fanfare for the argument.

Released as a single in April 1967, a month after the album, Tramp reached Number 26 pop and 2 on the R&B charts. There is nothing else quite as effective on the LP. A lively version of Eddie Floyd's 1966 hit Knock On Wood – Floyd says he and Steve Cropper originally wrote the song for Otis but Cropper cannot recall this being the case – got the album off to a fine start but their reading of Carla's 1966 hit Let Me Be Good To You lacks the communication of two people in the same place at the same time. It is clearly one of the four tracks to which Carla added her vocals after Otis's lead. Their mix of voices on the Sam And Dave hit When Something Is Wrong With My Baby works better than on their reading of the Aaron Neville hit, Tell It Like It Is. A raucous romp through The Clovers' Lovey Dovey, co-written by Atlantic founder Ahmet Ertegun and a hit in 1954, was cut at the same session as Knock On Wood and was released as a single after Redding's death. It reached 21 on the R&B list, 21 pop. New Year's Resolution, written by Stax staffers Mary Frierson and Randall and Deanie Parker Catron, was another track on which the singers recorded their vocals at separate sessions. The same was true of the rather flat and unexceptional remake of It Takes Two, a hit for Marvin Gaye and Kim Weston in January 1967, after it was lifted off the *Take Two* album, which had been released in the summer of 1966. Their duet on Are You Lonely For Me Baby? similarly lacks fire. But Otis's eternal fascination with the works of Sam Cooke ensures a meaningfully sung Bring It On Home To Me. The final track, Ooh Carla, Ooh Otis, written by Redding and Al Bell, has precious little to recommend it melodically and relies wholly on the impetus of the band's playing. Otis's voice, not for the first time, sounds tired, over-stretched and in need of proper rest.

The success of *King And Queen* encouraged the belief that a duet album would become a regular event for Otis each Christmas and the William Bell-Judy Clay song, Private Number, was reportedly written for the 1967 project. A duet album between Otis and Aretha Franklin had been discussed, which was something to think about indeed. Sadly, nothing came of it.

7 Soul Invasion – *Otis In Europe*

OTIS REDDING'S ADMIRATION FOR SAM COOKE stemmed from the soul star's singing and composing but there was no doubt that he also respected the way Cooke – and Ray Charles – had handled their business affairs. Few African-American artists had been able to exert a reasonable degree of control over their finances – though in this respect the music business was, to be fair, colour blind. Less than scrupulous managers, record company bosses and publishing houses would rip off anyone of any race, creed, colour or sex if they could; however, African-Americans had the extra indignity of seeing their work watered down in white cover versions and sold in great quantities to the mass white audience, enriching many people except the originators. Cooke, by and large, had avoided many of these pitfalls by establishing and building a relationship with a manager he trusted (J.W. Alexander), getting and keeping control of his own publishing and looking to the future by encouraging and nurturing other talent. Charles, too, had prospered financially when he quit Atlantic for an extra-ordinarily generous contract with ABC-Paramount, which allowed him to keep his own masters and set up his own label, Tangerine.

In 1965, as his success hit a new peak, Otis had taken a similar route. He had set up two companies, the Jotis Records production company and the RedWal Music publishing house, with the two businessmen with whom he had most dealings – the seasoned Joe Galkin, the man who had taken him to Stax, and his younger manager from Macon, Phil Walden. Jotis recorded just four singles – Loretta Williams, a singer from Redding's revue, did a version of Baby Cakes backed with I'm Missing You, before leaving the road show in 1966. Billy Young, a friend of Phil Walden's from the US Army service, cut a single and Arthur Conley, Redding's protégé, released two singles, neither of which hit. But after another two flops on Fame, both produced by Otis, Conley was switched to Atco and immediately found a smash. Based not too subtly on Sam Cooke's Say Yeah and namechecking the year's most popular voices, Conley's Sweet Soul Music, written and produced by Otis, stormed the charts to become a bigger hit than Redding had managed at that time, reaching Number 2 on the US pop charts in April 1967 and Number 7 in the UK a month later.

As to RedWal, the set-up made perfect sense. By now, Walden's agency had grown to become the biggest in the South, handling soul, R&B and blues acts. Otis was by no means its biggest draw. In 1966, Sam And Dave had hit the charts running and spun off four straight R&B Top 10 hits, one of which, Hold On! I'm Comin', reached 21 on the pop charts. They, too, were soon doing good business with Walden.

"Before Phil Walden," Sam Moore said, "there were a lot of hangers-on that promoted themselves – or the artists promoted them – from being go-fetch and alleged friends to being manager. When you do that, their character changes. All of a sudden, the manager becomes bigger than the artist. He's wearing the diamonds and the necklace and the shirt is open and he really becomes the top dog. And then I got with Walden. Phil didn't seek us out. We joined RedWal's booking agency to be booked and in the process we found out that he also had a management thing going. And we got caught up into that. Phil did a helluva job with Otis, no question. See, he didn't have Otis at first. It was Phil's brother, Alan, and Otis's brother Rodgers Redding. Both guys were in the service at the time. So when Rodgers left to go to the Army and Red [Alan Walden] had come out of the service, he started to manage. So when Phil came out of the Army himself, he had taken over the management of the agency. And, I'm gonna tell ya, he did a damn good job with Otis."

Arguably the greatest impact Otis Redding had on the road was not in the US at all but in Europe and Britain in particular. By the early '60s, the fire of rock'n'roll had been doused by watery cover versions, but when soul music started to be heard in Europe on American Forces radio and Radio Luxembourg, the recognition and appeal of the new music as a logical extension of R&B was immediate. Young British beat groups – The Beatles, The Rolling

Stones, The Kinks, The Who – started covering the songs, and the originators of the music began a shuttle service to tour Europe.

Otis Redding toured Britain twice. The most famous tour – the Stax/Volt tour of March and April 1967, when he topped a bill featuring Sam And Dave, Carla Thomas, Booker T. And The MG's, The Mar-Key Horns, Eddie Floyd and Arthur Conley, and which went on to stun Paris – was the first trip abroad for all but Otis. He had already been to Britain on a series of club and ballroom dates in the autumn of 1966. Barry Dickins, now head of International Talent Booking (ITB), was at that time a young booker at the London agency which handled the tour. "I was working for Harold Davison in Regent Street. Otis was one of the worst deals I ever did. I put him in the Orchid Ballroom, Purley, which is now called Tiffany's or something like that. Otis was getting £500 or £600 a night. The guy who was the manager said to me, 'I'll either give you £300 a night against a percentage or I'll give £650.' If I'd have taken a percentage he'd have walked out with about £1,500. That was one of my worst deals ever.

"Otis was the only act I've ever asked for an autograph – and still is. It says, 'To Barry, Respect, Otis Redding'. I know it's got a little tear on it. It was the Stax/Volt publicity photo, he's down on his knees, in fact it's quite a well-known picture. We played The Ram Jam Club in Brixton, that's where he signed it. I can remember that because I sat on the side of the stage watching. Fantastic. That's the sort of gigs he did. For some reason, I don't remember going up north with him. I just remember going around London. He just came in for a week. We may have played a ballroom in Lincolnshire, the Gliderdrome, Boston. I've got a feeling he played that. The guy who owned it, Sid Malkins, 'owned' Boston, Lincolnshire. He owned the football club, the cricket club, this massive place. It was like a Mecca ballroom but privately owned. Two thousand, three thousand capacity. Huge place.

"Harold Davison and Tito Burns, I think, did the deal. I was just like the gofer on the road. I remember we played a gig in Farnborough in Hampshire. It was a small place. The guy who booked it was a guy called Laurie O'Leary who ran The Speakeasy [a famous musicians' after-hours hangout near London's Oxford Circus] and he used to also book this club. We all went on the bus. Basically, it was a ballroom tour. It wasn't in the days when you played the Albert Hall and places like that. He went down well but the crowds weren't huge apart from the Orchid Ballroom in Purley, which was like his London show. That was the only place where there were thousands. This place in Farnborough was hundreds rather than thousands.

"It was there that Otis said to me, 'Can you tell me where the rest rooms are?', and I thought he wanted to lay down. I'd never heard of a toilet being called a rest room before." There were other small instances of culture clash. Like English food. "They hated it. That was another thing. Lemonade. 'Cos English lemonade is like R. White's [a particularly sugary, bubbly concoction] but in America it's made of lemons. And they always moaned about the sandwiches because every time they got a sandwich it had about this much ham in it [indicates the thinnest sliver]. In America, they were used to a triple-decker, three pieces of bread. Ninety per cent of the acts I dealt with in those days complained about that because we didn't have McDonald's in those days, Wimpy was the nearest we came to it. I remember he didn't have a rider [for pre-show refreshments in his contract], so I had to go out and buy 'em 12 Wimpys."

Redding did not use local pick-up musicians. "It was his band, not Booker T. And The MG's. One of the saxophonists was like the MC. Otis did a song I'd always loved, called One, I think. A great song, nobody else ever did it. I think Three Dog Night had a big hit with it in America, 'One is the loneliest number . . . ' [A Harry Nilsson song, it first appeared on the songwriter's 1966 debut, *Spotlight On Nilsson* – although there may be confusion here with Otis's own Your One And Only Man.] But I loved all those songs, Mr Pitiful. Of all the acts I've had, he's the one I know least about, probably. They played Ready Steady Go! I remember that."

Although not a strict disciplinarian, and well known for partying very heartily when the opportunities arose, as they often did on the road, Redding nonetheless demanded a certain amount of organisation. "Otis used to fine the band if they were late but I can't exactly remember who was. Some of them were pretty tough about getting up. I used to lie to them about picking them up. If it was a drive out of London, I used to say that I'd pick 'em up at eight and turn up at half past, even though we didn't have to leave until nine. But after about a week they sussed that out. So we were always late anyway." But Dickins is fairly sure the band was not fined James Brown-style for missing a lick on-stage. "I didn't see that but I wasn't privy, I didn't go in his dressing room when there was anyone else in there."

Essentially here for the TV exposure on RSG!, the tour was by no means sumptuously appointed or big on expenses. "They stayed in OK hotels but not the top, whereas if he was as big today as he was then he'd stay at The Mayfair or The Regent, The Savoy or The Dorchester. It wasn't in that league. They were making very little money, very little money, all travelling in the bus.

"Otis used to wear a very powerful deodorant. It was in a pinkish, reddy bottle. Used to slap it all over him. The equivalent of Brut in those days. Horrible. He was pretty normal, he wasn't over the top and, like I say, I was in awe of the guy. I was always, What do you want? I'll get you three of those, sir. He was pretty easy going, always very nice to me but at the same time he frightened the life out of me. I was always, Yes, Mr Redding. No, Mr Redding. He wasn't particularly tall but he was big. And he was quite athletic, he wasn't fat.

"I certainly don't remember him being difficult. I

don't have any memories of him being an arsehole. Ike Turner was different. We did Ike And Tina Turner after, which I can remember quite well because I actually went on the road with them for weeks and P.P. Arnold [one of The Ikettes] stayed behind and made that record, The First Cut Is The Deepest."

The first Otis tour opened Phil Walden's eyes to the potential for the music of the Memphis label in Britain and he immediately suggested a package tour, initially called Hit The Road Stax. Apart from a one-off show in Los Angeles, it was the first time such a label-wide show was to play outside Memphis and its environs. Walden put up the finance for it and booked the tour through promoter Arthur Howes. Studio musicians had to re-learn songs they had recorded one, two, three or four years before and dust off old stage moves. It was a timely tour with a tight schedule – a couple of days' rehearsal, a reception at the Bag O'Nails, a popular club in the West End of London, and two shows at the Finsbury Park Astoria (later known as The Rainbow Theatre) on Friday, March 17.

"I remember the long journey and then that first landing," said Booker T. Jones, digging deep into his memory. "The first shock I had was of talking with people, because when we went to a few clubs to hang out people were very friendly and they would tell us of the problems and the trouble they had in obtaining the music. And how they had to be practically courageous to go here and there to find the certain shops that would sell that kind of thing. So the fans were people who had gone to a lot of effort to hear the music. So that was pretty unusual for 1967."

"We were a bunch of kids having a great time with new movie cameras, not being able to believe we were going over so big with all the audiences," Wayne Jackson recalled. "The Beatles sent limos to pick us up from the airport and the reception we got was just . . . [gapes]. We went from session musicians making a hundred, two hundred dollars a week to screaming, superstar treatment. We were drunk when we arrived. I can remember all of us fighting to get through the door into the hotel lobby and the guys in the hotel handing out the keys. And then someone shouted out that the Queen was passing by and we all rushed out the door with cameras clicking at anything that moved.

"The reason the Stax/Volt package happened in the

first place was because of Jerry Wexler and Atlantic Records. Jerry put all that together and the reason he did was because he'd picked up the Stax option and all the artists on that tour were artists that Atlantic Records had and were promoting. Otis could have kept going back with his band, obviously, he was such a phenomenon. He didn't need Booker T. And The MG's and the Mar-Key horns to get over. He was a total phenomenon and Stax/Volt merely told me that what we had been doing for the last six or seven years had been significant to somebody and that Otis was here to stay. Sam And Dave too."

"When we were invited to perform with the Stax/Volt tour, we were only booked for maybe six weeks and we wound up staying here two, three months," Sam Moore added. "We came over here and we destroyed Europe with our music. We came over with all the guns. We had Booker T. And The MG's, as you well know, Arthur Conley had Sweet Soul Music, Sam And Dave had Hold On! I'm Comin'. Soul Man went gold when we were invited back by ourselves, we were in England at the time when it went gold. Carla Thomas, Eddie Floyd with Knock On Wood and Otis. So now you got a dynamite package. Small, not as large as Motown when they brought their thing over here, but we came over with our small package. And Europe has been very, very good to us over the years."

Unfortunately, not everyone deserving of the Stax/Volt trip made it. "When Otis went over on the tour David [Porter] and I couldn't go," Isaac Hayes recalled, with a note of considerable regret. "We had to stay back and mind the store and I hated that. God, I wanted to go so bad. But Booker [T. Jones] played, he played organ. But I coulda been there and played keyboards, too, 'cos I played on a lot of the tunes, but they didn't let me go."

Unlike many of the great soul packages of the mid-'6os, on their comparatively brief, whirlwind swings through Britain and the rest of Europe the Stax/Volt show was recorded live. Twice, in fact, at the Astoria in London and at the Paris Olympia, enough for an *Otis Redding Live In Europe* album, two volumes of *The Stax/Volt Revue*, one from Paris and one from London, *The Mar-Keys And Booker T. And The MG's: Back To Back* and a final dredging, *Stax/Volt Live In Europe Volume 3*. Booker T. And The MG's opened the first and second halves of each show. Then there were brief sets by The Mar-Keys and Arthur Conley before Carla Thomas closed the first half. Eddie Floyd went on next, before Sam And Dave did rather more than warm up the audience for Otis. When he came on, the crowds were smoking, whipped up by climax after climax of Moore and Prater's gospel-rooted call-and-response fervour. "Only thing we would focus on was doing a good show and getting the crowd to go into a frenzy," Sam Moore asserted. "Otis, Conley, Booker and Eddie and Carla also – we were focused just on doing good . . . we did seven [consecutive] nights sometimes and then had one night off just to travel."

One immediate result of the tour was Otis's elevation to Top Male Singer in the prestigious Melody Maker Readers' Poll. "I remember when he topped Elvis in the UK," Isaac Hayes agreed, "that was a big, big thing." Indeed, it was the first time Presley had been dislodged from the top spot for a decade.

Of course, Otis's hit records and his 1966 appearance on Ready Steady Go! had done much to pave the way for both the tour and his startling poll success. The Stax/Volt Revue, and the wild reviews of it, was another big step up the ladder. The tracks on the various live albums from the London and Paris dates reveal Otis Redding's performance, and indeed most of the revue, as a runaway train. Even more so than the *Live At The Whiskey A GoGo* sets, Otis's shows in Europe reveal him to be a dynamic live performer, a force whose music and personality reached out across the footlights, embracing the European audiences and briefly sharing his enjoyment of life with them.

"When we were there in '67, I had not played on-stage behind a performer who was so energetic and intent on pleasing the audience as he was. It meant so much to him," said Booker T.

Introduced by pirate radio DJ Emperor Rosko, who was MC in London, the band and Redding are soon heard blasting through Respect. Booker T. And The MG's and The Mar-Key Horns make far more accomplished accompanists than the road band heard at the Whiskey A GoGo. The set is intense from the start with Al Jackson's drumming and, particularly, Duck Dunn's bass being brilliantly propulsive. I Can't Turn You Loose stokes the blaze further, before I've Been Loving You Too Long (To Stop Now) leads the audience from rapt, pin-drop attention, via bursts of spontaneous applause throughout, to its pulsing climax. A faithful reading of his My Girl segues, via Jackson's pounding drums, into Shake. Satisfaction keeps the mood tumultuous thanks to the insistent drive of the MG's.

In the version of Fa-Fa-Fa-Fa-Fa from the Parisian show, Otis demonstrates his newly acquired grasp of French by inviting the audience to sing "Je t'aime, je t'aime, je t'aime . . ." where they had been singing "Fa-fa-fa". These Arms Of Mine – or "the big ol' arms of mine," as he sings – is next and then comes The Beatles' Day Tripper, breathlessly reinvented as a manic riffstorm, the new frantic, staccato version ending with horns, and Jackson and Dunn accompanying Otis's final emotional utterances. He introduces Try A Little Tenderness against a sea of excited cries and still rippling applause. Voices yell out requests: "Down In The Valley!" one cries. Another hollers for Pain In My Heart! But Tenderness brings down the curtain, and the house.

On *Live In Europe*, the London and Paris shows are mixed and matched, but the third volume of live action features the London show in close to its entirety. As such, it gives a much better picture of the dynamism of his set, with a valedictory Otis returning with the massed Stax choir of Carla Thomas, Eddie Floyd, Sam And Dave and Arthur Conley.

"We were shocked and elated at the reception," Wayne Jackson recalled, "but when we got back [to Memphis] we fell into the same groove of recording 'til eight, gig 'til 2am, one-hour jam perhaps and start over again at 11." Otis told Jim Delehant that he had "loved England from head to toe". The weather, oddly enough, appealed to him, as did the people. "So groovy. They treated me like a somebody." He thought that if he ever left the United States he'd live in England. But, he added, he'd never leave his Big O Ranch.

On March 21, while Otis was in Europe, back home Stax released one of his least successful singles, the Booker T. Jones and Eddie Floyd ballad, I Love You More Than Words Can Say, which reached only 30 on the R&B charts and 78 pop. A prolific writer for others, Jones did not provide much material for Otis. "We didn't write much together, one or two songs. It was always an idea that I had that he liked and could write a lyric or add a melody to. He never wrote to anything I played on the keyboards, he wrote to the guitar. The lyric ideas for the songs, in most cases it was Otis's."

I Love You More did not seem to interfere with the

sales of the Otis and Carla duet Tramp, which was released on April 13, shortly after his return. Two weeks later, a live version of Shake, recorded at the Finsbury Park Astoria, was in the racks and peaked on the R&B charts at 16 (47 pop). Also recorded by most of the Stax roster at this time were Stay In School messages and radio spots. With the drive to integrate schools in the South and to dismantle the other bulwarks of institutionalised racism, many soul artists from James Brown down stepped out on the freedom trail, and part of Stax's contribution was to record a series of tracks designed to encourage African-American children to take their education as far as possible. Otis's Stay In School had the highest profile and was the most successful.

Another great occasion that summer was The Redding Bar-B-Q. "Since he lived in Georgia I never went to his house," said Isaac Hayes. "He gave a party at the Big O Ranch one time in the summer of '67, he gave this huge barbecue. The Big O had a round swimming pool, the whole bit. It was nice, really nice. And a lot of the DJs and some of the artists went down to the party. He was just a well likeable person."

On June 30, a version of Billy Hill's Glory Of Love (19 R&B, 60 pop), a much-covered standard which had been a hit for Benny Goodman's jazz orchestra in 1936 and The Five Keys R&B vocal quintet in 1951, was released and a month later Otis and Carla's Knock On Wood was issued as a single, proving rather more commercial (Number 8 R&B, 30 pop).

But the most stunning event of the summer, of course, was Otis's appearance at the Monterey Festival, where, as we saw in the opening chapter, the huge acclaim he received seemed to open the floodgates to American crossover success on a scale to surpass even the triumphs of those European tours.

8 Madison, Wisconsin – *Dreams To Remember*

OTIS LOVED HIS "FARM", AS HE REFERRED TO the Big O Ranch outside Macon, Georgia. There, he raised "cattle and hogs" and liked to hunt on horseback. And it was there he returned when, after the Monterey Festival, he underwent the operation on polyps in his throat. As he waited for the wounds to heal, he planned with manager Phil Walden the best way to capitalise on the success of the European tour, the Monterey Festival appearance and steadily improving singles and album sales.

After six weeks of hoarse whispering that followed the operation, Otis went back into the studio to cut new tracks and to revisit songs he'd recorded one, two or three years before – ones that had never been finished to his liking. In a frantic three-week spate of activity at the end of November and beginning of December 1967, he recorded the material that would provide the bulk of three post-humous albums and a subsequent caravan of outtakes and alternative versions. It's immediately evident from the new recordings that his voice is in better shape than for many years and that during his enforced "holiday" he had been giving serious thought to the future direction of his music. There can be no greater evidence of this than his biggest hit, (Sittin' On) The Dock Of The Bay.

Written while he was in California, the ruminative ballad has become his epitaph, a more potent memento than any of the great ballads that established him in the R&B market (Pain In My Heart, These Arms Of Mine, I've Been Loving You Too Long), the proud soul thumpers (Respect, I Can't Turn You Loose) or the idiosyncratic remakes (My Girl, Satisfaction, Try A Little Tenderness). Dock Of The Bay signalled a fundamental change in Otis Redding's style. The song has an accessible melody that did not require Redding to stretch high or reach low, and lyrics which contemplate the universal subject of longing – for a better, brighter tomorrow – while accepting whatever fate has to offer, accepting that things might indeed remain the same until the times were ready for a-changing. There is no evidence, other than his participation along with almost the entire Stax/Volt roster in the Stay In School promotion, that Redding was in any way a political animal. But just as he would try songs by The Rolling Stones or The Beatles when they were shown to him, the lyricism in songs by writers like Bob Dylan, despite having "too many words", clearly had caught his attention.

"I know in my own mind it was the best thing we ever did with him," Steve Cropper said. "Otis and I knew we had something when we wrote it but when we recorded it we said, 'This is it, this is the song we've been looking for, this is the one that's gonna cross us over.' The way he sang it was just awesome. When you do it for a living like we do, there are times when you think you've got something and there are times when you know you've got something. The only thing we didn't do was add The Staple Singers. It may not have worked but we were going to try that."

Many of those who heard Dock Of The Bay – Phil

Walden, Jim Stewart – were doubtful about it. "I remember (Sittin' On) The Dock Of The Bay," said David Porter. "Otis was in town to record and he asked me to hear this new song he'd written and he came into my office and strummed it to me. I was able to offer some advice, which he took, and that was to make the first verse the last verse and the last verse the first."

Dock Of the Bay wrapped up the three-week recording binge which had proved that Redding's voice was now fully recovered.

Otis and The Bar-Kays got ready to leave on a short tour starting the weekend of December 8–10, 1967. It was back to business as usual. "I can recall that last trip that he made," Isaac Hayes said. "We was all hanging out in the lobby, not the studio, and his pilot Dick said to me, 'Man, why don't y'all come go with us'. They wanted me and David to go with them. And we were going but Sam And Dave were in town for a concert so we said, 'No, we can't go, man, 'cos Sam And Dave are here and we got to go see 'em, 'cos they were our artists and we got to be supportive'. He said, 'We're going to Nashville, Cleveland, Madison, Wisconsin'. 'Well, yeah, but we got to hang back.'"

Trumpeter Ben Cauley had lately joined Otis's road band, The Bar-Kays. "I had been in the studio cuttin' with the Memphis Horns first. Then I went out on the road with Otis. He was a groovy cat, like an older brother. He looked after us all." The young Bar-Kays were in their teens but already a lot was expected of them as a Stax band for the future. They were from River Arrows and had been in the Memphis area since 1966. "We were very close together and it showed on-stage, very tight. He was very spontaneous but we didn't change too much from how the songs had been recorded, the arrangements. But he got a really good groove, kept us together." At one time, Otis had used a 10-piece band on the road but the line-up was now down to eight – two trumpets, two tenors, organ, guitar, bass and drums.

After the show in nearby Nashville, the entourage flew up to Cleveland, Ohio for an appearance on a local TV show, Upbeat, presented by Don Webster, and later in the day played the second concert of the weekend. Otis called home early on the morning of December 10 and promised to ring again when they arrived at Madison, Wisconsin for the final show of the short trip. But the call would never come. At 3.28 on the afternoon of Sunday, December 10, 1967, Redding's private Beechcraft came down in the freezing dark waters of Lake Monona, four miles from Madison Municipal Airport. The plane hit the lake with tremendous force, wildly scattering debris. Otis, his pilot and five of The Bar-Kays' entourage were killed. Cauley survived. "It's not really hard to talk about now. At first it was. I really . . . we had just woke up. The airplane started shakin' and I can remember the sax player was sittin' in front of me and he said, 'What's that?!' and then, 'Oh no!'"

On impact, Cauley was flung out of the Beechcraft, still in his seat, and, as he couldn't swim, he held on to a cushion and floated while all around him the stunned group members, and Otis, who liked to sit up front with the pilot, drowned. Of the group, Cauley was the only survivor. Bassist James Alexander was not on the flight but guitarist Jimmy King, keyboard player Ronnie Caldwell, saxophonist Phalon Jones and drummer Carl Cunningham all perished with Otis. Divers were still searching the bottom of the lake for bodies on Tuesday, December 12.

"We cried," Isaac Hayes said for everyone at Stax. "It was such a shock. Because he was a person that represented so much life. When they're gone it's like, 'What do we do?' We just sat around. When we got the news, everybody came to the studio. We just sat around. It's hard to describe it. And, of course, along with him, the loss of The Bar-Kays, too. Jimmy King, guitar, who started off with me in a band. I was like his mentor. Little Carl Cunningham was Al Jackson's protégé, but I call him my son because he used to hang with me and 'Bowlegs' Miller at the Four Ways, we used to feed him all the time. Phalon and Ronnie, the keyboard player, and Matthew Kelly was like their valet, he lived right down a couple of doors from Stax in this apartment block. It just stunned Memphis, so many lives lost at one time."

David Porter, rather than being in town to hear a Sam And Dave concert, remembers it slightly differently. "I was with Booker T. And The MG's at the time. We were out of the city working on the college circuit when we heard. I called home and spoke to my wife. All she had heard on the radio was there had been a crash and some people thought it was us. But she said later they announced it was Otis, so I was the one who took it back to Steve and Booker and Duck. I was just numb on the plane back to Memphis.

And then a little later, the funeral, well that was a very sad experience."

Booker T. remembers it, too. "Without a doubt. We were at the bar in Cincinnati. We were about to fly home. And Al Jackson's wife found us in a bar at the airport and told us. We had played at some club or something in Cincinnati and . . . yes, well, we had to fly home with that knowledge."

Otis Redding's funeral was held on December 19 in Macon, Georgia. Six thousand mourners turned out and stars crammed in. "I didn't go to the funeral," Hayes said. "I didn't want to remember them like that. And it was a fiasco anyway, people, fans was just . . . Joe Tex had to run for his life, I believe, because they were charging at the entertainers. It was just a shock and a tremendous loss.

"And nobody thought of it in terms of the monetary losses, you know, the records that we weren't selling. It wasn't that. It was this strong life force, the energy that he gave off that warmed so many people. It was like he was our hero and he was not a pretentious person. He didn't try to be more than what he was. You know when a person starts to reach fame and fortune they try to become a bit snooty and stuff like that. But he was always down to earth. Always. He'd sit down and eat baloney and crackers with us, or like I said we'd go to Four Ways and get some soul food. And he always liked to have an idea and sometimes we worked all night. I've slept under the piano many nights, on the floor. Nobody would refuse to work with him. He would be the driving force. Sometimes you'd be like, 'Phew' [wipes brow in tiredness] and he'd be 'C'mon, guys, let's go! Let's go!'"

It was a tragedy that touched the entire African-American music industry and caused no little unhappiness among music fans at large. In his ghosted autobiography, The Godfather Of Soul, James Brown recalled their last conversation, a few days before the fatal crash, in which he says he cautioned Otis against learning to fly his twin-engine Beech 18. He also warned Redding that the plane was not big enough to carry "all those people and all that equipment". "Somebody was fooling Otis," Brown continues. "They tried to do the same thing with his twin-engine that I did with a Lear jet, and they couldn't do it. That plane was an old plane, with a bad battery and a lot of service problems, and it had no business flying in that kind of weather."

"The last time I spoke to Otis I was joking with him about training for his pilot's licence," Stax songwriter and recording artist Eddie Floyd said at the time. "I will never forget that day – he wasn't flying himself but he died in his own plane. I can only say that I've lost my brother. We as soul brothers are as one. He wasn't the only one . . . there was the great Sam Cooke . . . I don't even know my own destiny."

Two days after Otis's death, Jim Stewart called the staff of Stax Records into the studio on McLemore and said that they just had to try to accept and forget the great tragedy and get on with the business of recording hit records. "It was never the same without Otis," David Porter said. "He was such an integral part of everything and it was not possible that it could be the same."

"It wasn't until then that we realised the stature he had in the family," Booker T. said, "and how you can take people for granted. It made us realise how important Otis had been to Stax as a person and as a musical figure. But he was good friend to everybody, everybody liked him."

"When Otis died there was a big rush to get the best of the latest stuff out there," Steve Cropper remembered.

"[After that] I don't think I listened to another Otis record until 1973 or 1974 ... it was too hard for me ..."

"Dock Of The Bay was a bittersweet success because it was almost prophetic," Hayes said. As Hayes spoke about Otis's death his eyes filled. "He wrote about Dock Of The Bay and he died, crashed, in a place called some kind of bay or something. But anyway, it was so prophetic. And lyrics like 'So many people try to tell me what to do, I guess I'll remain the same'. I don't know what the real deal was but somebody might have been trying to tell him to change his image or something but he didn't want to change it and I think those lyrics came out as Dock Of The Bay. Just like when Albert King did a tune called Cold Feet, he was pissed off behind the mic. 'Everybody talkin' 'bout, git your cold feet off me woman, tell me tryna sing like Sam And Dave and Johnnie Taylor ...'. It was something that got Al pissed off and you would think that he was doin' that as a gimmick on a record but he was serious. So, I'm sayin' that I think that Otis, I think he had some frustrations when he did Dock Of The Bay. He was expressing them in the lyric."

"It took me a while to get it back together," the surviving Bar-Kay Ben Cauley said with a very large side order of understatement, "but eventually the only thing was to put the group back together and press on with it, press on with our lives and the music." This The Bar-Kays did to very good effect, forging new styles and sounds in keeping with the changing times. "We saw something in them that we couldn't even project ourselves," MG's drummer Al Jackson once said. Guitarist Steve Cropper agreed: "I think basically we saw ourselves all over again. But they started at a much higher level."

Cropper felt that with such a monumental personality as Redding's gone, everyone at Stax worked that little bit harder to try to replace a little of what the company had lost. The late Al Jackson agreed and added, "We realised we could never replace Otis so we spent all the time really trying to make a William Bell, trying to make a Johnnie Taylor, to take up the slack and all that we lost in Otis."

9 Amen

OTIS REDDING DIED LESS THAN THREE MONTHS after his glorious triumph at Monterey and barely five years after his first R&B chart entry. His passing meant he was never able to explore the route pencilled in by his newer, mellower music, epitomised by the posthumous hit (Sittin' On) The Dock Of The Bay, which would go on to win Best R&B Song and Best R&B Performance at the 11th Grammy Awards in March 1969.

In the success of Dock Of The Bay there was yet another echo of the life and career of Sam Cooke, who also died young, shot dead by a jealous woman. Just before his murder, he too had suggested a newer, more philosophical and reflective turn to his music with A Change Is Gonna Come. Redding's death, however, had repercussions which reached much further.

"I think now that Stax Records died with Otis," Wayne Jackson said. "We had a little group of people, we didn't even realise this, that we were a fraternity. A young, little group all dedicated to having fun, and that fun was the music we were doing. Otis, Sam And Dave, all the artists up to 1967. Stax continued, they kept making records but it got more and more uncomfortable as the fame of it grew and Isaac Hayes became a big star and Isaac got into the big money, the pop money. And then the gangsters started hanging around, with guns, and it didn't feel fun anymore. It wasn't fun. So me and Andrew left. Booker T. left. Steve Cropper left. Duck left. The bones got up and walked. Then they had imitators, hangers-on, leeches, power struggles, big companies trying to buy something that no longer existed. Paramount, Gulf-Western, CBS, the FBI, the CIA, everybody was involved. It was the shadow of a race car that used to really run good. People were buying and selling the memory of it for big dollars."

Booker T. saw the business evolution at Stax as

something that owed most to "the type of mentality that came into the United States when a company developed a new machine, a new technology, and became really large. It was the first time I had encountered that type of thing. Gulf-Western bought Paramount Pictures and soon after Paramount Pictures bought Stax and that was an unheard-of thing, to me. Previously, it had been more like the Japanese way of doing business, that if you were in a company you were in it for life and the company's your company from when you're born to when you die.

"And so that shook it up. There were memos sent out from New York about ways to do business and corporate decisions were made that we had to abide by that were just foreign. It just was not the Delta, Memphis, Southern blues type of creative energy that was necessary for our way of doing music. We started to have meetings and board rooms! It shifted away and I saw the shift so I just threw my hands up and moved away. And the shift was legal, there was contracts signed and money exchanged, the whole thing, so some of that was good in that the company had good finance. But the way of working changed completely – we were given shifts. [The MG's] had a shift and The Bar-

Kays had a shift and they were looking for a third band for a shift. That may have been what did it. I just thought, 'All I have to do is go to the airport and get on a plane [to Los Angeles]'. Not a move I regretted, I would have been swallowed up in the corporate thing."

At the side of the Stax building that faced on to College, at the back of the site, there was once a set of large electric gates that you passed through when turning into the studio's small parking lot. It was here, in 1969, that Wayne Jackson and Andrew Love finally decided they'd had enough.

"They were searchin' my and Andrew's horn cases every time we went in and came out, people who didn't know who we were. There were so many people in there stealin' whatever they could get their hands on, microphones, anything, so they were even searching us and we were [some of] the motherfuckers that had started the deal. So there were people here who didn't know who we were, who were treating us badly and carrying guns down the hall.

"And Andrew and I stood right on this spot [in the former parking lot], spun the cap off a half pint of bourbon

– it was summer time – passed it back and forth, if you will, and I said, 'I'm gonna go in there and tell Jim Stewart I wanna cash out. What d'you think, do you wanna take our chances against the world? We can do it anywhere, and they don't want us to, they don't want us to do it anywhere else but here. We come here, we get treated badly and they don't pay us enough.' Andrew said, 'Fuck him! Do it!' So I went inside and told Jim that we just didn't believe that we could do it anymore so he gave us our little paycheck for that week." Jackson's voice moderates to little more than a whisper. There is still a great sadness at the memory of what the label had and lost.

For a while, the likes of Johnnie Taylor and The Staple Singers kept the flame alive, kept preaching the faith. "Isaac Hayes was still out there, bald-headed and chained like he was, Black Moses and all that horseshit, but it was selling a lot of records. But what you liked about the records that we made, what we liked about the records that we made, died with Otis around about that time. Not just because of his death. But because it signalled something. The heart and soul was gone. Although the horns were still there, Booker T. And The MG's were still there, we still made good records for another year or two. After that, it began to break down."

Jim Stewart began to lose control of – or interest in – the situation at Stax and Al Bell took over more of the day-to-day running and planning. "I sometimes wonder what it would have been like had [Otis] lived," Jackson mused, "what direction it would have all taken had he lived because he was just starting to kick. He was real smart. Phil [Walden] was pretty smart but Otis was real smart on his own two feet, all by himself."

Of the tracks recorded by Otis Redding in what turned out to be his final sessions, four were hit singles after (Sittin' On) The Dock Of The Bay in 1968 (The Happy Song Dum-Dum-De-De-De-Dum-Dum, Amen, Hard To Handle and I've Got Dreams To Remember), while A Lover's Question, Love Man and Free Me charted in 1969. The Happy Song is Redding and Steve Cropper's obvious riposte to Fa-Fa-Fa-Fa-Fa (Sad Song). Like Dock Of The Bay, it is much more lambent and reflective in mood, as though slow days and long nights back at The Big O Ranch during his recuperation from the polyps operation had made him a contented man. It was also the final Otis Redding single released on Volt under the old distribution agreement between Stax and Atlantic. The remainder were released on Atco, the label which had been releasing his albums.

Again, he returned to Sam Cooke for inspiration and sustenance, recording the traditional gospel song Amen, staple of many a soul singer's live show, in an arrangement which shadows that of Sam Cooke's as heard on the *Live At The Copa* album. He sings a chorus a cappella, before introducing the horns and then the rhythm section, essaying a final chorus all together before using two verses of This Little Light Of Mine and then returning to Amen. It is a noticeably understated performance by comparison with the recordings in the 12 months before his operation. In July and August of 1968, Amen was a double-sided R&B hit with Hard To Handle, written with Al Bell and Allen Jones, who would later find greater fame as producer of the later generation of The Bar-Kays. Hard To Handle, a better-seller in the pop market and a UK Top 20 hit in August and September, 1968, was recorded earlier in the three-week spell. Otis seems to have been exploring the scope and range of his post-operative voice on a song which sounds – particularly through the a cappella lines at the end of each verse and the number of words in each line, more than Redding was usually comfortable with – as though it was originally intended for a singer like Joe Tex.

The most spellbinding of the new singles was I've Got Dreams To Remember, co-written with his wife Zelma. For only the second time, Redding is heard with backing singers, added after his death, as he recounts the cautionary tale of catching his wife kissing a friend "again and again and again". With Cropper's spatial chording, Booker T's churchy organ chords, Dunn's spare bass playing and Jackson limited to off-beat snaps of the hi-hat, the heat is very gently increased. His performance of this pensive song, more than any other track he recorded in these last sessions, points towards Dock Of The Bay.

His live version of James Brown's Papa's Got A Brand New Bag, recorded at the Whiskey A GoGo, was a Top 10 R&B hit single at the very end of 1968, while March 1969 saw another Top 20 R&B hit with his version of Brook Benton's A Lover's Question, despite it having one of the least successful rhythm arrangements – improbably jaunty and making a plain pitch for the pop market. Love Man, a Number 17 R&B hit in May 1969, is a brusquer return to his macho stomp-and-strut style but the lyrics suggest a nod to the "Love Crowd", as he had called the Monterey audience. His description of the Love Man as six feet one inch tall and weighing in at 210 pounds might be close to autobiography, but the "long hair and pretty fair skin" was not by any stretch of the imagination. Free Me, his last R&B hit, reached Number 30 in August 1969. A soul ballad, it struck a better balance between the poppier stance of his new melodies, which the horn lines subtly magnified, and the soulful content of the older style, exemplified by Cropper's guitar and Redding's gently pleading delivery.

The 1968 singles, except (Sittin' On) The Dock Of The Bay and Papa's Got A Brand New Bag, formed the basis of *The Immortal Otis Redding*, the first posthumous album, which was released in June 1968. Of the other tracks, You Made A Man Out Of Me, written by Deanie Parker, an artist-turned-writer and Stax's head of publicity, and Steve Cropper, was a solid, steady four/four, while Redding's own Nobody's Fault But Mine again sounds as though he had been listening carefully to Joe Tex's Dial recordings. His ballad, Thousand Miles Away, opens promisingly but the idea of love trying to span distance is underdeveloped lyrically and the melody and arrangement sound unfinished. Better by far is his sincere reading of Think About It, co-written with Don Covay. Phil Walden's wooing of his future wife lit the spark for Champagne And Wine, written by his brother Alan, Roy Lee Johnson and Redding. As with many of the tracks from this time, this ballad sounds more like a demo than finished product – there is a hesitancy about the playing that would not have survived a final session. Finally, Ray Charles's A Fool For You is subjected to a typical Staxation.

A year after *Immortal*, another batch of posthumous releases appeared on Love Man. His repetition of "ya ya" places I'm A Changed Man, written with Cropper, in the Sad Song/Happy Song genus, but it spoils an auspicious mood and melody. The uptempo That's A Good Idea, in which Otis decides that the way to a woman's heart is to let her have everything she wants, is melodically thin; he is on much more solid ground on the ballad I'll Let Nothing Separate Us. Another collaboration with Cropper, Direct Me is again slyly observant about his past – he's been crying for five long years, he sings, which is just about the time from the start of his hits to the final recording sessions –

while the funkier rhythm to Groovin' Time recalls the work of New Orleans's great soul studio band The Meters, slippin' and tippin' behind Lee Dorsey. Of two final solo compositions, Your Feeling Is Mine sounds unfinished, while Got To Get Myself Together is more considered. A version of Jackie Wilson's (Your Love Has Lifted Me) Higher And Higher are briskly kicked along by Al Jackson's drums, Duck Dunn's bass, and jolly horns but Redding's singing reveals little. His merry take on The McCoys' Look At That Girl, another rarity with backing vocals, is one of the most blatantly commercial of the posthumous album tracks and very frolicsome to boot.

In 1970, a third posthumous release, Tell The Truth, collected 12 more tracks – three cover versions, six solo compositions and three collaborations, one of which is often disputed as being co-written by Redding. Johnny's Heartbreak, credited on the album to Otis and Arthur Alexander, the Southern soul singer who wrote Anna, You Better Move On, Every Day I Have To Cry and Go Home Girl, reappeared much later on Alexander's 1993 album Lonely Just Like Me as Johnny Heartbreak, in a typically country-tinged performance. In both versions the song sounds immeasurably more like Alexander's work than Otis's. Shortly before his death in June 1993, Alexander commented that he'd been "tickled" that Otis had recorded the song "before he made it big". It is unclear whether Alexander was "tickled" that Redding had used the song or "tickled" at Otis's part appropriation of the publishing rights. Certainly, in later years Alexander claimed to have written the song alone. The other cover versions are less controversial. The title track is a fine version of The Five Royales' 1958 recording, there is a straightforward pulse through James Brown's Out Of Sight, and the third cover version, of Little Richard's Slippin' And Slidin', is one of the oddest and least successful Otis ever tried.

Of the rest, Demonstration, written with Don Covay, is a simple extension of the Love Man ethic, here offering "love" demonstrations. The Match Game, written in 1966 with inveterate puffer David Porter, squeezes as many flammable words and images as possible into the lyric, but doesn't quite catch fire. Of the six originals, Give Away None Of My Love is sung with great energy and the rhythm section's drive is all that's expected, but the song seems empty at heart. Wholesale Love opens with a loud and untuneful voice yelling by Otis's side which somewhat sets the scene – despite the good arrangement his singing is ragged on a work of demo-like quality. The pop changes in the verses of I Got The Will contrast with the soulful sign-off at the end of the last line of each verse. A Little Time is little more than a collection of previously heard lines – melody and lyric – put together in working-draft fashion, although Otis sings them with great gusto and belief. Snatch A Little Piece and Swingin' On A String likewise give the impression of songs that would benefit from a little more work.

Although Otis's recorded legacy is comparatively small, many subsequent hitmakers have been clearly influenced by him from Arthur Conley to reggae star Toots Hibbert. Even such an unlikely cove as Peter Gabriel – lead singer of progressive rock band Genesis and solo world music explorer – imitated Redding when he was trying out his voice at Charterhouse public school.

In the wake of Redding's death came several tribute records, most notably William Bell's Tribute To A King. "A fantastic song," Steve Cropper admitted to Rolling Stone. "I dig this song, not because I loved Otis alone – Otis deserved Tribute To A King because he was King, King Of Soul, King Of Stax, and King Of Everything that evolved around us. If you just listen to the lyrics in that song, they tell that whole story. I've been writing for years and I would never have been able to get all that information in three minutes. No way could it be done, but Booker came up with it."

Of course, there has also been much revisionist writing on the works and singing of Otis Redding, and many have argued that as a singer he was over-rated. He did not have the shading or suppleness of Sam Cooke, and too easily became a parody of himself, the classical form of the early ballad performances later steamrollered by coarse phrasing. Whatever one's opinion on the merits of his singing, I do not think that anyone seriously doubts that he was a major soul songwriter.

Take his most famous song. Like Wilson Pickett's In The Midnight Hour, Eddie Floyd's Knock On Wood and Aretha Franklin's version of Respect, (Sittin' On) The Dock Of The Bay is redolent of a period and a culture. But more than that, its mood of contemplation, its atmosphere of quiet yearning mixed with an easy satisfaction have made it a universal, generation-hopping favourite. Many of the soul acts of the '60s have found that the great songs which made their names became a millstone around their neck, setting them in a certain time, unable to move on. Would Dock Of The Bay have become a millstone for Otis, a barrier to progress? I doubt if he'd have let it become so. Percy Sledge faced that potential problem when When A Man Loves A Woman gave him a hit in 1966 with his first record.

"I've been doing that for nearly 30 years," he said. "I know what they want to hear. They want to hear When A Man Loves A Woman so I always do all of my great hits and do that last. Of course, I've done that two or three times in a show, but I always do it last. It's a great feeling, too, to have a song like that, when people love it so much. It gives you more strength, power, like it generates."

April 20, 2001. Back at the razed site of 926 East McLemore Avenue, a crowd of some 3000 has gathered to witness the start of another dream to remember. Following years of stagnation, and then months of negotiation and toil by Soulsville Inc, a non-profit group, the land has been bought back from the Church Of God In Christ. And now fans, musicians and local dignitaries are gathered together to take part in a jubilant groundbreaking ceremony in preparation for the construction of a $20 million Stax Museum Of American Soul Music and Stax Academy And Performing Arts Centre.

The project, coaxed along by Soulsville Inc president Deanie Parker, the one-time Satellite Records store worker who became Stax press officer, songwriter and recording artist, has, in the words of Steve Cropper, been a long time coming. But with an opening date roughly pencilled in for the summer of 2002, there is genuine optimism that 926 East McLemore Avenue could once again become the hub of a busy, vibrant and productive community – that's how strong the echo of Otis's legacy is.

Timeline

SEPTEMBER 9, 1941 Otis Redding born to Fannie and Otis Redding Sr.

1944 Family – he also had four sisters and one brother – moved to Macon, Georgia.

1958 Goes on the road as a stand-in Little Richard to fulfil the Georgia Peach's itinerary with The Upsetters. Enters and wins DJ Hamp Swain's Teenage Party talent shows at the Douglass Theatre, Macon. Winning several consecutive weeks, he meets future wife Zelma, Johnny Jenkins and his manager Phil Walden.

JULY 1960 Goes to Los Angeles, records four tracks (She's Alright, Tuff Enuff, I'm Gettin' Hip, Gamma Lamma).

SUMMER 1961 Back in Macon, records Shout Bamalama and Fat Girl.

AUGUST 1961 Marries Zelma.

FEBRUARY 1962 Johnny Jenkins And The Pinetoppers, including Otis Redding, record Love Twist for local label, Gerald. It is licensed for national distribution by Atlantic.

OCTOBER 1962 Redding drives Jenkins and fellow Pinetoppers to Stax Studios in Memphis for Atlantic session to record Jenkins's follow-up. Redding uses spare time at the end of the disastrous session to record Hey Hey Baby, in his customary Little Richard style, and his own soul ballad, These Arms Of Mine.

DECEMBER 1962 These Arms Of Mine released on the Stax subsidiary Volt. It will reach Number 20 on the US R&B charts and 85 on the pop charts.

JUNE 24, 1963 That's What My Heart Needs recorded. Reaches 27 on the US R&B charts.

SEPTEMBER 26, 1963 Pain In My Heart, freely adapted from Allen Toussaint's Ruler Of My Heart, recorded in Memphis. Released in October, it will peak at 61 on the pop charts.

NOVEMBER 1963 Otis makes his debut at the New York Apollo.

JANUARY 16, 1964 Records Security, which will become his fifth Volt single when it is released on April 24. Peaks at 97.

FEBRUARY 1964 His first album, *Pain In My Heart*, is released. On the 6th he records his fourth Volt single, Come To Me. Released later in the month, it reaches 69 on the pop charts.

MARCH 1965 Second album, *The Great Otis Redding Sings The Soul Ballads*, is released and will top out at Number 147 on the US pop lists.

APRIL 19, 1965 Single version of the great soul ballad I've Been Loving You Too Long, co-written with Jerry Butler, is released and in June/July reaches Number 2 R&B, Number 21 pop.

JULY 9, 1965 Otis with Booker T. & The MG's and Stax's favoured horn section featuring Andrew Love and Wayne Jackson finish recording *Otis Blue* album in concentrated sessions.

AUGUST 5, 1965 The mono single version of Respect is released and will reach Number 4 R&B and by October crosses over to hit 35 pop.

JANUARY 1966 My Girl, the UK choice as single from *Otis Blue*, is Redding's chart debut reaching 11.

MARCH 1966 *Otis Blue* starts a 21-week run in the UK charts, topping out at Number 6.

APRIL 1966 *The Great Otis Redding Sings The Soul Ballads* makes the UK LP charts and goes up to 30.

APRIL 9–10 Redding's performances at the Whiskey A GoGo in Los Angeles are recorded but the live album will not be issued until after his death.

JUNE 1966 Releasing *The Soul Album* (54 US pop, 22 UK pop), Otis also launches his Jotis label, whose roster includes Arthur Conley. His Otis-penned Sweet Soul Music will reach Number 2 in the US and Number 7 in the UK in 1967, bigger hits than Redding achieved in his lifetime.

OCTOBER 1966 *The Otis Redding Dictionary Of Soul: Complete And Unbelievable* is released in the US and will reach 73 on the pop charts. Released in January '67 in the UK, it makes 23 pop.

FEBRUARY 1967 A re-released *Otis Blue* makes 7 in the UK LP charts.

MARCH 17, 1967 Otis plays the first date of a Stax/Atlantic UK package tour at the Finsbury Park Astoria with Booker T. & The MG's, The Mar-Keys, Sam and Dave, Eddie Floyd, Carla Thomas and Arthur Conley.

JUNE 1967 Otis records duet album with Carla Thomas, *King And Queen*. Tramp, the first single, makes Number 26 in the US pop charts.

JUNE 17, 1967 Otis plays the Monterey International Pop Festival, closing the second night. Following Jefferson Airplane, he wins over the white rock audience completely.

AUGUST 1967 In the US, *Otis Redding Live In Europe* is released. It will reach 32 on the pop charts.

DECEMBER 6 AND 7, 1967 Having spent two months recovering from an operation for the removal of polyps on his throat and getting his voice back into shape, Redding records the basic tracks for (Sittin' On) The Dock Of The Bay.

DECEMBER 9, 1967 With his backing band The Bar-Kays, Otis leaves Memphis for live dates in Nashville, Cleveland and Madison.

DECEMBER 10, 1967 Flying into Madison, Otis's twin-engine Beechcraft plunges into Lake Monona. The singer, all but two of The Bar-Kays, the pilot and road manager perish.

JANUARY 8, 1968 (Sittin' On) The Dock Of The Bay is released in the US. It will reach Number 1 and stay there for four weeks. In the UK it reaches Number 3.

Bibliography

Booth, Stanley, *Rythm Oil* (Jonathan Cape, 1991)

Bowman, Rob, *Soulsville USA* (Books With Attitude/Schirmer, 1997)

Charles, Ray and Ritz, David, *Brother Ray* (Macdonald & Jane's, 1979)

Fox, Ted, *Showtime At The Apollo* (Quartet, 1983)

Gillett, Charlie, *Making Tracks* (Souvenir, 1988)

Guralnick, Peter, *Sweet Soul Music* (Harper & Row, 1986)

Hirshey, Gerri, *Nowhere To Run* (Times Books, 1984)

Lydon, Michael, *Ray Charles: Man And Music* (MOJO Books, 2000)

Wexler, Jerry with David Ritz, *Rhythm And The Blues* (Jonathan Cape, 1994)

White, Charles, *The Life And Times Of Little Richard* (Pan, 1985)

Wolff, Daniel, *You Send Me: The Life And Times Of Sam Cooke* (Virgin, 1996)

Also many magazines including MOJO, Black Music, Rolling Stone, Blues And Soul, Jet, Melody Maker, New Musical Express, Goldmine, Record Collector and the many soul fanzines that continue to spread the word.

Discography

United Kingdom

SINGLES

Pain In My Heart/Something Is Worrying Me (London) January 1964

Come To Me/Don't Leave Me This Way (London) April 1964

Mr Pitiful/That's How Strong My Love Is (Atlantic) April 1965

Shout Bamalama/Fat Girl (Sue) April 1965

Respect/I've Been Loving You Too Long (Atlantic) August 1965

My Girl/Down In The Valley (Atlantic) November 1965

(I Can't Get No) Satisfaction/Any Ole Way (Atlantic) April 1966

My Lover's Prayer/Don't Mess With Cupid (Atlantic) July 1966

I Can't Turn You Loose/Just One More Day (Volt) Dec 1965

Fa-Fa-Fa-Fa-Fa (Sad Song)/Good To Me (Atlantic) November 1966

Try A Little Tenderness/I'm Sick Y'All (Atlantic) January 1967

Day Tripper/Shake (Stax) March 1967

Let Me Come Home/I Love You More Than Words Can Say

(Stax) April 1967

Shake (live)/634–5789 (live) (Stax) June 1967

Tramp/Tell It Like It Is (with Carla Thomas) (Stax) July 1967

The Glory Of Love/I'm Coming Home (Stax) September 1967

Knock On Wood/Let Me Be Good To You (with Carla Thomas)
(Stax) September 1967

(Sittin' On) The Dock Of The Bay/Sweet Lorene (Stax) February
1968

Lovey Dovey/New Year's Resolution (with Carla Thomas) (Stax)
March 1968

The Happy Song (Dum Dum)/Open The Door (Stax) May 1968

She's All Right/Gamma Lamma (Pye International) June 1968

Amen/Hard To Handle (Atlantic) July 1968

I've Got Dreams To Remember/Champagne And Wine
(Atlantic) October 1968

Papa's Got A Brand New Bag (live)/Direct Me (Atlantic)
December 68

A Lover's Question/You Made A Man Out Of Me (Atlantic)
March 1969

Love Man/That's How Strong My Love Is (Atco) June 1969

Free Me/Your Love Has Lifted Me Higher (Atco) August 1969

Look At That Girl/That's A Good Idea (Atco) February 1970

Wonderful World/Security (Atlantic) July 1970

Merry Christmas Baby/White Christmas (Atco) Oct 1968

ALBUMS
The Great Otis Redding Sings Soul Ballads (Atlantic) September 1965
Otis Blue: Otis Redding Sings Soul (Atlantic) March 1966
The Soul Album (Atlantic) July 1966

The Complete And Unbelievable: The Otis Redding Dictionary Of Soul (Atlantic) January 1967

Pain In My Heart (Atlantic) April 1967

The King And The Queen Of Soul (with Carla Thomas) (Stax) July 1967

The History Of Otis Redding (Stax) December 1967

Otis Redding In Europe (Stax) March 1968

The Dock Of The Bay (Stax) June 1968

The Immortal Otis Redding (Atlantic) August 1968

In Person At The Whiskey A Go Go, Los Angeles (Atlantic) November 1968

Love Man (Atco) August 1969

Tell The Truth (Atco) January 1971

Live At The Monterey International Pop Festival (with Jimi Hendrix) (Reprise) 1971

The Best Of Otis Redding (Atlantic) July 1973

Dock Of The Bay: The Definitive Collection (Atlantic) 1993

The Very Best Of Otis Redding (Atco) 2000

United States

SINGLES

She's All Right/Tuff Enuff (with The Shooters) (Transworld, also on Finer Arts) 1960

I'm Gettin' Hip/Gamma Lamma (Alshire) 1960

Shout Bamalama/Fat Girl (Confederate) 1961, second pressing (Orbit) 1961, reissued (Bethlehem) 1963, reissued (King) 1968

These Arms Of Mine/Hey Hey Baby (Volt) Oct 1962

That's What My Heart Needs/Mary's Little Lamb (Volt) June 1963

Pain In My Heart/Something Is Worrying Me (Volt) Sept 1963

Come To Me/Don't Leave Me This Way (Volt) Feb 1964

Security/I Want To Thank You (Volt) April 1964

Chained And Bound/Your One And Only Man (Volt) Sept 1964

Mr Pitiful/That's How Strong My Love Is Dec 1964

I've Been Loving You Too Long/I'm Depending On You (Volt)
Apr 1965

Respect/Down In The Valley (Volt) Aug 1965

I Can't Turn You Loose/Just One More Day (Volt) Dec 1965

(I Can't Get No) Satisfaction/Any Ole Way (Volt) Feb 1966

My Lover's Prayer/Don't Mess With Cupid (Volt) May 1966

Fa-Fa-Fa-Fa-Fa (Sad Song)/Good To Me (Volt) Sept 1966

Try A Little Tenderness/I'm Sick Y'All (Volt) Nov 1966

I Love You More Than Words Can Say/Let Me Come Home
(Volt) March 1967

Tramp/Tell It Like It Is (with Carla Thomas) (Stax) April 1967

Shake/You Don't Miss Your Water (Volt) April 1967

The Glory Of Love/I'm Coming Home (Volt) June 1967

Knock On Wood/Let Me Be Good To You (with Carla Thomas)
(Stax) July 1967

(Sittin' On) The Dock Of The Bay/Sweet Lorene (Volt) Jan 1968

Lovey Dovey/New Year's Resolution (with Carla Thomas) (Stax)
Jan 1968

The Happy Song (Dum Dum)/Open The Door (Volt) April
1968

Amen/Hard To Handle (Atco) June 1968

I've Got Dreams To Remember/Nobody's Fault But Mine (Atco)
Sept 1968

Merry Christmas Baby/White Christmas (Atco) Oct 1968

Papa's Got A Brand New Bag (live)/Direct Me (Atco) Nov 68

A Lover's Question/You Made A Man Out Of Me (Atco) Feb 1969

When Something Is Wrong With My Baby/Ooh Carla, Ooh Otis
(with Carla Thomas) (Atco) April 1969

Love Man/I Can't Turn You Loose (Atco) April 1969

Free Me/Your Love Has Lifted Me Higher (Atco) July 1969

Look At That Girl/That's A Good Idea (Atco) Nov 1969

Demonstration/Johnny's Heartbreak (Atco) March 1970

Give Away None Of My Love/Snatch A Little Piece (Atco) July
1970

I've Been Loving You Too Long (live)/Try A Little Tenderness
(live)

ALBUMS

Pain In My Heart (Atco) Jan 1964

The Great Otis Redding Sings Soul Ballads (Volt) March 1965

Otis Blue: Otis Redding Sings Soul (Volt) Aug 1965

The Soul Album (Volt) April 1966

The Complete And Unbelievable: The Otis Redding Dictionary Of Soul
(Volt) Oct 1966

The King And The Queen Of Soul (with Carla Thomas) (Stax) March
1967

Live In Europe (Volt) Aug 1967

The History Of Otis Redding (Volt) Nov 1967

The Dock Of The Bay (Volt) March 1968

The Immortal Otis Redding (Atco) June 1968

In Person At The Whiskey A Go Go (Atco) Nov 1968

Love Man (Atco) June 1969

Tell The Truth (Atco) July 1970

Live At The Monterey International Pop Festival (with Jimi Hendrix) (Reprise) Aug 1970

The Best Of Otis Redding (Atco) Aug 1972